Commission of the European Communities
D.G. XXIII Tourism Unit

# TAKING ACCOUNT OF ENVIRONMENT
# IN TOURISM DEVELOPMENT

1993

ECONSTAT

This final report has been carried out by
a research group of Econstat composed by:

- Stefano Dall'Aglio (project coordinator)
- Gilberto Zangari
- Giorgio Pirrè
- Giancarlo Gasperoni (field researches coordinator)
- Isabella Malagoli  (data management)

This report and the outcomes of the research are due to the
common analysis and discussion.

A central support for the completion of this  study has been
given by the professionals who have conducted the analysis of
the case histories in different countries (see the annexes of the
study):

- G. Gardner Smith (case history: Eastbourne, UK)
- A. Annyfanti(case history: Corfu, Greece)
- C. Altes (case history: Lloret de Mar, Spain)
- P. Borjan (case history: Knokke Heist, Belgium)
- J. Capella Hereu (case history: L'Estartit, Spain)
- P. Paolinelli (case history: Costa Gallura/Costa Smeralda, Italy)
- G. Zangari (case history:Rimini, Italy)

# INDEX

# TAKING ACCOUNT OF ENVIRONMENT IN TOURISM DEVELOPMENT

## 1. FOREWORD

Tourism activity, more than other economic sectors, uses environmental resources as main inputs into its "production function".

For the most part, such resources are non-reproducible and play a fundamental role in determining a destination' appeal to tourists; but their use and modifications also have decisive impact on an area's social and economic development beyond its prospects as a tourism product.

In accordance with the OECD report -- *L'impact du Tourisme sur l'Environment*, 1980 -- the environmental resources which most need special attention are:

1. acquatic *milieu* (streams and rivers, seas, coastlines and coastal waters, water fauna and flora);
2. natural *milieu* (soil, forest fauna and flora, landscapes, air);
3. architectural milieu (man-made constructions, which attract tourists because of their peculiarity);
4. human *milieu* (human activities, which can be experienced independently from their objective or the context in which they are carried out).

This notion of environment was still limited to meanings linked to "relevance for tourists". The last two points were emphasized solely for the aspects perceived by tourists, whereas no mention is made of internal aspects, invisible to the tourist but of extreme importance for the local area's growth and the success of tourism investments (in terms of social tension, labour market, property and land values, etc.).

Therefore, we are currently led to define 'environment' as that vast array of factors which represent external (dis-)economies of a tourism resort: natural (air, water, soil, wildlife, climate), anthropological, economic, social, cultural, historical, architectural and infrastructural factors which represent a habitat onto which tourism activities are grafted and which is thereby exploited and changed by the exercise of tourism business.

In this broad sense, environmental consciousness of tourist demand is growing fast and has become one of the prime determinants of holiday travel destination choice.

Today, such "environmental motivations" of the tourist - which are also the tourism entrepreneur's "economic motivation" - has rendered private operators (local hoteliers, ground operators, tour operators), local and national authorities, and even the local community more aware of and sensitive to the problem. All these actors are more conscious than in the past about the opportunity of protecting the environment in which tourism activities take place: the safeguarding of the environment and its balance is a necessary condition for mid- and long-term tourism growth.

At the same time, the market success or failure of a tourism destination ends up returning considerable feedback to the surrounding environment in terms of "signs" on the territory, impacts on nature, modification of social, cultural and economic conditions. As the WTO/UNEP report (1983) indicates, these effects can even be beneficial in that tourist spending may engender an economic motivation in favour of environmental preservation.

The determination of the relationships between the environmental situation and the appeal of a tourism destination is therefore the priority goal of this study. The proposal deals with both the effects on the environment caused by the tourism development and the effects of the environmental situation on the competitiveness of the resort. These two relationships interact with each other, too often in a vicious circle, and end up determining the resort success or failure on the market and, in the ultimate analysis, the debasement or the upgrading of the local environment.

Of course, one must distinguish between *short-term* effects and *mid-long term* effects, the latter usually being more pervasive as well as more difficult to recognize and control.

As a recent study has underlined (Econstat. *Tourism and Environmental Crises: the Impact of Algae on Summer Holidays along the Adriatic Riviera in 1989*, Esomar, 1991), to a certain extent (and in specific cases) in the short term the environmental crises can be counterbalanced by a good combination of good tourism factors (service quality, variety of leisure activities, artificial equipmen, hospitality, competitive prices...), while the long-term crisis poses a serious challenge to the livelihood of the local tourism industry.

The tourism industry must become more aware of the environmental factor and is able to do so by preparing and implementing effective solutions in the management of resources both internal to the development projects and external to them.

The acknowledgement of the factors affecting the relation between tourism development and the environment is the objective of this study.

5

# 2. RESEARCH METHODOLOGY

## 2.1. INTRODUCTION

From the beginning of the 70's tourism demand has undergone a formidable growth process and an increase in territorial diffusion. The accelerating trend manifests itself worldwide involving all active, and even potential, resorts.

Besides important positive results, this tendency has also had undesirable effects:

- on still undeveloped areas where the environmental "system" is under pressure;

- on traditional tourist resorts, many of which have entered a declining phase, partially as a result of environment deterioration.

In recent years the environment -- in its multifaceted meaning of natural elements, socio-cultural values for the local community, production input for tourism activities -- has become a primary factor in the creation, development and management of tourism resorts.

The macro-trends of tourist demands assign a growing importance to environmental factors: the quality of tourism supply (and environment is actually the main factor of tourism supply) is becoming a discriminating criterion in the choice of the holiday resort.

The tourist is increasingly attracted to resorts which provide an escape from the problems and discomforts of everyday living: noise, intense traffic, parking problems, traffic jams, and all other aspects connected with urban living.

These negative effects are present in almost all seaside resorts developed during the "mass tourism " phase, and are beginning to make the difference. They probably contribute to the decline which today characterizes many of these situations .

The deterioration of the environment may not only be the cause of loss of competitiveness of a resort in the tourism market, but may be the effect as well.

As long as there are economic opportunities in the resort, part of the profits can be employed for the upkeep of the environment.

When competitiveness decreases it can lead to a process of environmental deterioration:
decreased competitiveness -> decreased prices -> decreased income and return on investments -> lack of resources for maintenance and rebuilding -> slowing down of retraining in the services sector -> fewer work prospects for the young and tourism workers -> environmental deterioration -> decreased competitiveness etc.

At the same time there are cases of resorts in phases of decline in which the creation of new economic opportunities and new perspectives for the tourism operators have determined an environmental retraining.

In the near future at global level this request for "environment" will increase, the tourist will be more selective and experienced and environmentally friendly products are expected to be more successful than other; for the same reason, products which don't have even the minimum of environmentally compatible standards are expected to decline and lose competitiveness.

Therefore a series of interventions are needed:

- <u>at new tourist areas</u> where development should be carried out in a "sustainable" way i.e. must be realized in a way that is compatible with the local environment (natural resources, social and cultural values of the host population, etc);

- <u>at older tourist resorts</u> through stimulation of a revitalization process answering the needs of the mass consumer but at the same time adopting measures and starting projects with the aim of up-grading the local environment.

Nevertheless it must be noted that in such situations the private and public actors who play a role in tourism development often have long standing interests for which they tend to avoid change. For this reason the renovating/retraining process becomes difficult and sometimes impossible to start autonomously.

Our work will focus on tourism resorts which are already well advanced in their life cycle, which have "consumed" environmental resources in the past and which <u>are losing</u> or <u>have lost</u> or <u>are regaining</u> competitiveness on the tourism market.

The market for tourism in the third millenium, in fact, will consist of "environmentally friendly" tourism products that don't require too much compromise on performance and value. These changes will take place regardless of the greater costs implied by environmental conservation and restoration.

The future of resorts which were developed in a mass-oriented tourism context depend on re-thinking and recovering in a "soft" way situations which are compromised (i.e., environmentally incompatible). The above-mentioned mass-oriented context is the major obstacle for such a new growth policy.

Success in imposing environmental priorities in interventions concerning mature or declining resorts is instrumental in weakening pressure on areas which are (still) undeveloped or undevelopable for tourism.

The main objectives of the study are:

- to find out the possible actors, private or public, which can play either a positive or negative role in any process of environmental retraining;

- to identify actions, interventions, incentives, projects in order to support "sustainable" tourism development or relaunching strategies.

We believe that some of the novelty in this approach lays in the attempt to identify the possible promotors of tourist development as well as the reasons for their actions and examples of initiatives.

The detailed aims of the research are:

1) the identification of the actors, both public and private, both enterpreneurial and social, who have manifested sensitivity to environmental issues in tourism recovery;

2) the orientation of these subjects toward economic and tourism development of the area;

3) a survey of main actions and interventions carried out in the field of tourism in order to regain competitiveness or in order to renovate environmental conditions, developed by:
   - economic operators
   - institutional bodies
   - host community

4) the determination of factors or events favouring the actions mentioned in the previous point.

5) tourist evaluation of environmental evolution and reaction to the measures carried out.

6) host population evaluation of environmental evolution and intervention priority.

The study aims to define the pattern of relationships between environment and tourism competitiveness through the analysis of selected tourism resort case histories in different European countries.

## 2.4.1 Identification of resorts

To identify the tourist resorts/areas on which researches was carried out the following criteria were considered.

>    a) position on life cycle
>    b) type of resort

### a) we have focused the analysis on tourist areas in the maturity or declining or revitalizing stage of its lifecycle.

> This means that the selected resort are in one of the positions labeled A, B, C, D or E in the following figure.

> A reconaissance was performed in order to select at least one case for each of these positions on the life cycle curve.

We can summarise the reasons for linking the relations between tourism and the environment to the "resort life cycle" curve in the following points:

a. *the priority of mature areas.* Resorts in the maturity or decline phase have a high concentration of human and capital resources. The mixture of interests, resources and the agents involved makes interventions aimed at improving the environment as urgent as those aimed at protecting or controlling development in resorts at the beginning of the life-cycle curve.

b. *the environment as resource and the environment as product.* Is a resort's entry into the decline phase due to an inevitable decline in terms of the model of acceptance - choice - purchase of any product on the part of the consumer or caused by high consumption of environmental resources in the development phase?

c. *the impact of tourism development on environmental resources.* Each phase of the life cycle has a corresponding degree of impact on the system of environmental resources (in the widest sense). When, if at all, does the need for control or limits on the impact of tourism arise?

d. *the agents involved in the tourism - environment relationship.* Who are the important agents (both positive and negative) in the various phases of the life cycle? What role to they play and how do they intervene?

e. *environmental resources and revitalisation.* How does the improvement of environmental resources figure in the overall revitalisation of a declining resort?

1 0

These are all questions of great importance if we are to understand the relationship between tourism development and the environment, and it is to these problems that we will attempt to give a reply.

## Tourism Life Cycle

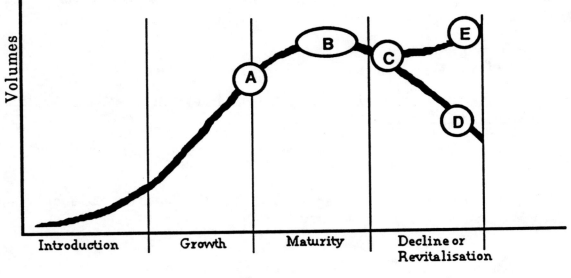

b) <u>we have decided to concentrate the analysis on seaside resorts.</u>

Due to the low number of cases dealt with, we thought it wold be more effective to concentrate on "homogeneous" resorts, i.e., from one tourism type only. In fact the problematic areas, the factors, even the actors and their involvement are very different in a seaside resort with respect to a mountain or rural resort.

Case histories were chosen based on the fact that awareness of tourism recovery had already been manifested through projects which also affect -- positively or negatively -- the environmental situation.

---

7 case histories  were carried out:

- Knokke Heist - Belgium
- Eastbourne - UK
- Corfu - Greece
- Rimini - Italy
- Riviera Gallura - Italy
- L'Estartit - Spain
- Lloret de Mar - Spain

---

## 2.4.2 Research Stages

The research has been divided into 3 stages (or separate sub-studies):

### A) DOSSIER ANALYSIS

The core stage has been carried out by means of gathering information on the basis of a dossier. The dossier was completed for each one of the resort areas selected. The basic information for the completion of the dossier was gathered through: interviews with local experts and representatives of institutions and private associations, etc. (see "Instructions for Completing the Dossier").

*See annexes for the case history analysis*

### B) SURVEY OF HOST POPULATION

In 2 of the selected resorts (Rimini, L'Estartit) additional surveys were conducted by means of direct interviews with the host population in order to analyze:

- its perception of the changes which have taken place at the local level
- the measures and initiatives to be undertaken to improve the environmental conditions
- a general evaluation of environmental awareness.

*See annex for the results of the surveys in Rimini and L'Estartit*

### C) SURVEY OF TOURISTS

In 2 of the selected resort (Rimini, L'Estartit) additional surveys were conducted by means of direct interviews with tourists in order to analyze:

- its perception of the changes which have taken place at the local level
- the measures and initiatives to be undertaken to improve the environmental conditions
- a general evaluation of environmental awareness.

*See annex for the results of the surveys in Rimini and L'Estartit*

In the following pages the main features of each resort studied are given.

# 3. PRESENTATION OF THE CASE HISTORIES

| RESORT | RIMINI ( I ) | EASTBOURNE (UK) | LLORET DE MAR (E) | L'ESTARTIT (E) |
|---|---|---|---|---|
| EXTENTION OF AREA (sq. Km) | 134.5 | 44 | 49 | 65 |
| TOTAL RESIDENT POPULATION | 128.000 | 81.000 | 15.000 | 6.900 |
| WHEN TOURISM ACTIVITY STARTED | 1850 | 1800 | 1960 | 1960 |
| RATIO TOURISM BEDS/POPULATION | 0,50 | 0,12 | 2,08 | 0,37 |
| WEIGHT OF TOURISTIC SECTOR ON LOCAL ECONOMIC SISTEM | 25% | 17% | 100% | 44% |

## TOURISM DEMAND

| | RIMINI ( I ) | EASTBOURNE (UK) | LLORET DE MAR (E) | L'ESTARTIT (E) |
|---|---|---|---|---|
| · ARRIVALS (,000) | 1057 ('90)  450 ('70) | 280 ('90)  381 ('66) | 82 ('87)  sharp decrease | 17 ('91)  20 ('85) |
| · BEDNIGHTS (,000) | 6300 ('90)  6500 ('70) | 1680 ('90)  3810 ('66) | | -  ( - )  ( - ) |
| · % ARRIVALS FROM ABROAD | 18% | 9% | | 83% |
| · % BEDNIGHTS FROM ABROAD | 17% | | 5% | |
| · SEASONALITY (% MAY - SEPT) | 73% | 70% | 66% | 89% |
| · % ORGANIZED TOURISTS | 16% | 25% | 90% | 39% |
| · IMPORTANCE OF EXCURSIONISTS /WEEKEND | very relevant | relevant | very relevant | relevant |
| · RELEVANT SEGMENTS OF TOURIST DEMAND | SUN & BEACH 65%  LEISURE-DISCO 17%  MEETING 3%  FAIR 2% | SUN & BEACH 65%  LANGUAGE STUDY 14%  BUSINESS 11%  MEETING 1% | SUN & BEACH 60%  LEISURE DISCO 28%  MEETING 5%  SPORT 5%  CULTURE 2% | SUN & BEACH 65%  SPORT 25%  CULTURE 2% |

## TOURISM SUPPLY

| | RIMINI ( I ) | EASTBOURNE (UK) | LLORET DE MAR (E) | L'ESTARTIT (E) |
|---|---|---|---|---|
| · N° OF HOTEL | 1504 ('90)  1633 ('70) | 281 ('90)  377 ('88) | 203 ('90)  191 ('88) | 33 ('92)  36 ('72) |
| · N° OF BEDS IN HOTELS (,000) | 64 ('90)  65 ('70) | 10 ('90)  12 ('70) | 31 ('90)  12 ('70) | 2 ('92)  2 ('72) |
| · AVERAGE SIZE OF HOTELS | 39 | 36 | 154 | 76 |
| · N° OF BEDS IN OTHER ACCOMM. (,000) | 60 | 10 | 31 | 8 |

## OWNERSHIP

| | RIMINI ( I ) | EASTBOURNE (UK) | LLORET DE MAR (E) | L'ESTARTIT (E) |
|---|---|---|---|---|
| · % LOCAL OF INVESTORS / TOTAL | 85% | n.a. | 70% | 100% |
| · % OF BIGGEST OWNERS / TOTAL | 35% | 25% | 80% | 75% |

| RESORT | KNOKKE HEIST (B) | CORFU (G) | COSTA SMERALDA (I) |
|---|---|---|---|
| EXTENTION OF AREA (sq. Km) | 57 | 592 | 618 |
| TOTAL RESIDENT POPULATION | 31.000 | 99.477 | 50.763 |
| WHEN TOURISM ACTIVITY STARTED | 1860 | 1975 | 1965 |
| RATIO TOURISM BEDS/POPULATION | 0,11 | 0,28 | 0,55 |
| WEIGHT OF TOURISTIC SECTOR ON LOCAL ECONOMIC SISTEM | 35% | 60% | 80% |
| **TOURISM DEMAND** | | | |
| • ARRIVALS (,000) | - (-) | 396 ('90) 128 ('70) | n.a. |
| • BEDNIGHTS (,000) | 2722 ('90) 3402 ('70) | 3471 ('90) 739 ('70) | n.a. |
| • % ARRIVALS FROM ABROAD | 5% | 76% | very low |
| • % BEDNIGHTS FROM ABROAD | 5% | 88% | very low |
| • SEASONALITY (% MAY - SEPT) | 75% | 82% | 71% |
| • % ORGANIZED TOURISTS | 1% | 75% | 5% |
| • IMPORTANCE OF EXCURSIONISTS /WEEKEND | very relevant | not relevant | not relevant |
| • RELEVANT SEGMENTS OF TOURIST DEMAND | SUN & BEACH 70% HEALTH, RELAX 23% CONGRESS 5% SPECIAL INTEREST 2% | SUN & BEACH 95% | SUN & BEACH 85% SPORT 10% GOLF 2% CONGRESS 2% |
| **TOURISM SUPPLY** | | | |
| • N° OF HOTEL | 76 ('92) 120 ('70) | 272 ('92) 55 ('70) | 32 ('92) 27 ('89) |
| • N° OF BEDS IN HOTELS (,000) | 3 ('92) 7 ('70) | 28 ('92) 3 ('70) | |
| AVERAGE SIZE OF HOTELS | 49 | 103 | |
| N° OF BEDS IN OTHER ACCOMM. (,000) | 69 | 48 | 60 |
| **OWNERSHIP** | | | |
| •% LOCAL OF INVESTORS / TOTAL | 75% | 90% | 10% |
| • % OF BIGGEST OWNERS / TOTAL | 30% | 10% | 90% |

| | RIMINI ( I ) | EASTBOURNE (UK) | LLORET DE MAR (E) | L'ESTARTIT (E) |
|---|---|---|---|---|
| **CHARACTERISTICS OF ACCOMMODATION FACILITIES** | Accommodation facilities are composed mainly of small family hotels | Accomodation facilities are almost all small and medium sized hotels | Accommodation facilities are characteristicly large locally owned hotels | Accommodations facilities are substantially of para-hotellerie i.e. holiday homes and campsites. There are also many large hotels |
| **PROBLEMS OF COMPETITIVENESS** | • revitalize "sun&sea" tourist supply<br>• spread tourist activities throughout the year<br>• Improve general competitiveness of tourist system | • low appeal of the resort<br>• traffic and parking problems<br>• rundown buildings | • loss of competitiveness<br>• the competitiveness of the resort is based on low prices<br>• the prices are too low and therefore tourist services are poor<br>• imbalance between prices of accomodation supply and other tourist services | • obsolete tourist supply due to the fall in investiment<br>• disproportion between prices of accomodation supply and other tourist services<br>• little adaptation of supply services to the present demand |
| **MARKETING STRATEGIES PURSUED** | Improve the quality of "sun and sea" tourist services<br>Diversify demand segments<br>Improve the quality of urban life | Defend the urban quality and aesthetic characteristics of the city<br>Diversification of the demand towards: elderly segment short breaks | Widening of tourist services<br>Demand diversification<br>Strong use of promotional and advertising activities | Stress on the environmental connotation of the resort<br>Improvement of the quality of the tourist supply directed at sun-sea tourism |

| | KNOKKE HEIST (B) | CORFU (G) | COSTA SMERALDA (I) |
|---|---|---|---|
| **CHARACTERISTICS OF ACCOMMODATION FACILITIES** | There is a clear predominance of individually owned holiday homes | There are many large hotels and non-hotel accommodations | Holiday houses and apartments built by a few big companies predominate |
| **PROBLEMS OF COMPETITIVENESS** | • Increasing competition for main holidays of sun & beach destinations<br>• Increasing urbanisation of the resort by buildings which are too high<br>• traffic and parking problems<br>• low occupancy rate of accommodation facilities<br>• little cooperation between the operators which obstructs the development of coherent and effective marketing strategies | • lack of infrastructure<br>• ruthless competition between tourist companies<br>• dependence on few markets<br>• concentrated seasonality<br>• construction without planning permission<br>• pollution | • lack of local organizations' territorial and economic plans<br>• lack of an entrepreneurial class<br>• traffic and parking problems in high season<br>• extremly short high tourism season |
| **MARKETING STRATEGIES PURSUED** | Qualitative improvement of the urban environment (traffic and parking places)<br>Requalification of tourist attractions<br>Development of new tourist products and demand diversification<br>Protection and qualification of natural attractions | Qualification of tourism services<br>Recovery from urban decay | Development of tourist structures and infrastructures |

# LOCALIZATION OF CASE HISTORIES

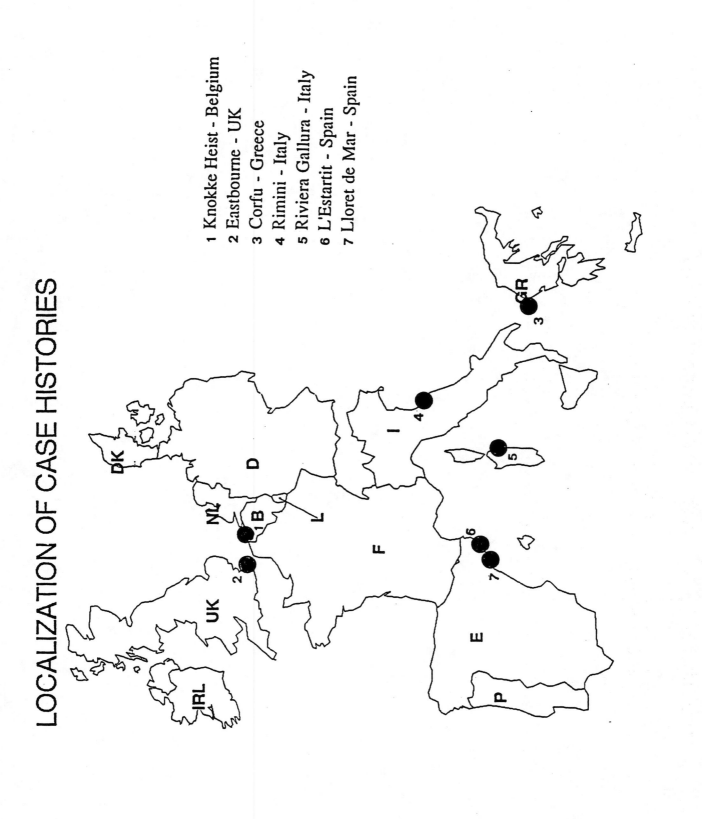

1 Knokke Heist - Belgium
2 Eastbourne - UK
3 Corfu - Greece
4 Rimini - Italy
5 Riviera Gallura - Italy
6 L'Estartit - Spain
7 Lloret de Mar - Spain

# 4. THE EFFECT OF TOURISM DEVELOPMENT ON THE ENVIRONMENT

## 4.1. INTRODUCTION

This chapter will examine in detail the relationship between tourism and the environment as observed in the resorts analysed (see Chap.3). We have taken "environment resources" to indicate the whole range of non-economic factors characterising an area which have an influence on tourists and have an effect on their satisfaction. This definition of environment includes various factors which taken together may influence the tourist's desire to return to a given area: natural resources (the quality of the sea water or the attractiveness of the countryside), the hospitality of the local people, local traditions, the presence of well-preserved works of art or historical monuments and so on. The framework for this research thus divides environmental resources into three broad categories:

1      - the natural environment

     The whole range of natural resources: land (beaches, mountains, etc.), air, water and their combination (countryside), fauna and flora. The natural ecosystem is without doubt the most delicate and the most difficult to control of the different environmental resources.

2.     - the social and cultural environment

     The entire set of traditions, customs, history, art, hospitality and culture that characterise a given area. This category includes the overall social climate of the area in which tourist activity takes place (the relationship between the local people and tourists, the presence of marginal groups, social tensions of various sorts).

3.     - the urban environment

     This category, which we may also call the "artificial environment", includes the transportation and communications infrastructure and in general all the services for residents as well as for tourists.

Obviously the tourists will not maximise their utilities from the simultaneous use of all three environmental typologies , nor will the supply facilities of all tourist areas be able to contemporaneously satisfy the demand for different types of environment. Broadly speaking, a seaside holiday on an exotic island will tend to satisfy a strong demand for the natural environment, a less strong one for the artificial environment and little demand as regards socio-cultural factors. A summer mountain holiday will tend to emphasise the natural environment but also the socio-cultural one, with a relative disregard for artificial aspects. A visit to cities famous for their artistic attractions involves in particular the socio-cultural and artificial environments and is more or less indifferent to natural aspects.

The seaside holiday in areas such as those considered in this study tends to satisfy demands on the level of the artificial environment, some of the natural environment demands but few of those regarding the socio-cultural environment. This is due in general because the "classic" or "hard" tourism development model -- that gives the base paradigma for such resorts -- doesn't allow for a relevant interaction between customer satisfaction and socio-cultural environment (see also K.H Rochslitz, 1986). An additional factor is that the resorts analysed are at a mature stage of their life-cycle and, at a general level, it seems there is a quite homogeneous nature of the relationship between tourism and environment in the various phases of the life-cycle of a seaside resort.

It is possible to distinguish at least four phases in this model, characterised by a progressive shift of the principal feature of attraction away from the natural to the artificial environment.

1) in the market entry phase the emphasis is on natural aspects;

2) in the second phase are introduced features of attraction concerning human activity ;

3) in the third phase, the artificial aspects become the most important feature of attraction;

4) finally, these artificial aspects become the feature that most characterises the tourist resort. In this final stage, the natural resources of the area are so marginal that they represent only one among the many attractions offered to the tourist.

The following sections will analyse the effect of tourism development on the environmental resources according to the broad definition given above. Particular attention will be given to the interaction between tourism development and the contextual variables, highlighting:

- negative effects
- positive effects
- long-term effects

Some concluding remarks will be made in each section in order to underline those aspects which emerge most frequently from the different resorts. In fact these constitute structural constants of tourist activity, and can be found throughout the study, both in "old" holiday resorts and in more recent ones, whether developed by local investment or foreign capital. A large part of these constants concerns in particular the effects of the interaction between tourism and the environment, and their identification constitutes one of the first results of this study.

### 4.2.1 Negative effects

- serious modifications of the coastal ecosystem (fauna, flora, morphology);

- intensive urbanisation of the area, degradation of the countryside;

- speculative pressure on agricultural land with the aim of rendering it suitable for building;

- sea pollution, algae and abnormal seaweed growth ;
  Due above all to the lack, shortage or inefficiency of the purification systems of urban waste.  This, however, is not always due entirely to tourist activity.  The pollution of the sea is often, and sometimes predominantly, due to urban, industrial and agricultural waste.

- coastal erosion
  This, too, is not always the fault of the tourist industry. It can also be occasionaly caused by the building of commercial or service structures (tourist ports, jetties etc.).

- air pollution;
  Car traffic constitutes the principal factor in the pollution of the air.

- excessive water consumption with respect to the capacity  of local supplies;

- pollution of ground water;
  This problem can be found in varying degrees in many Mediterranean resorts, and is caused by the lack or inadequacy of purification plants.

### Comments

The principal and most apparent negative effects of tourism development can be found in the sea water.  In the high season in particular, there is a tendency to overburden the water collection and purification plants (which are often inadequate), and it is thus common to find sea pollution problems of varying degrees near the main tourist areas. The degradation of the area concerns both the coastal and inland areas. Tourist investments tend to transform once and for all the ecosystem of the coast, whose fragile equilibrium can be severely damaged even by relatively small interventions.  Damage to the countryside is often due to major building works which are often not regulated and sometimes actually illegal.  Building affects not only the areas of the coast nearest the sea but also the inland areas, progressively affected by land speculation.  The latter, apart from losing their original characteristics, also no longer carry out the function of environmental safeguard.

Environmental degradation, then, slowly affects increasingly large areas, with environmental damage of different types which in time come together to give rise to highly complex and interrelated problems. The high season can sometimes give rise to an excessive use of water reserves and thus increase the risk of pollution due to the coming together of two separate dangers: the rise of the pollution of the untreated reflux water and the possibile infiltration of sea water. In some cases, although the drinking water is not actually polluted, there is nevertheless a decrease in quality due to the necessity of submitting it to an intense purification treatment.

In the urban areas, there is almost always considerable pollution due to car traffic, in particular in moments of greatest tourist activity.

If tourist activity takes place in an area in which there is other economic activity, the interactions between the economic system and the environment become even more complicated, with possible negative effects on the tourist industry itself.

The surveys show that tourism development can combine with other productive activities sometimes with difficulty, as the latter can result in a decrease in the competitivity of the resort itself:

- the presence of industrial activity often gives rise to a decrease in the quality of the air and a worsening of traffic problems.

- the construction of a commercial port can modify sea currents and thus alter or impair the sand of the beaches used for bathing.

- livestock breeding and agriculture lead to the dumping of polluting substances or fertilisers in the sea which worsen the quality of the sea water.

An area which intends to diversify its productive structure in order to reduce the excessive dependency on tourism should thus evaluate very carefully the sectors and firms it wants to encourage.


4.2.2 Positive effects

Occasionally, the tourist development of an area has given rise to actions aimed at environmental conservation either of the area itself or of nearby areas. This has been the case even in areas with very different characteristics in terms of the age of the resort, the tourism structures or the organisation of property. This tendency can be observed when the environmental value of an area (particularly the beauty of the countryside, the presence of rare animal or plant life, etc.) becomes itself the principal attraction of the resort. In this case, there is often concerted action on the part of those involved in tourism in the area to preserve and improve the quality of the environment. These interventions sometimes result in the creation of nature parks, but more often the problem of safeguarding the environment of the resort is not faced up to in its entirety, the principal objective being that of providing a "tourist attraction".

The case history made in the UK (Eastbourne) constitutes an important exception in that there are here specific plans to preserve even the urban landscape by means of the preservation of architectural style and urban organisation.

In the resorts where tourism development is particularly tied to features of the natural environment, the "tourism culture" of the local populace would seem to include the "environmentalist bug". Sensitivity to environmental issues, that is, can be seen to have spread first amongst economic agents and only later amongst the local inhabitants, the reason being that the environment has become an important economic resource.

A final observation concerns the oldest resorts. These were among the first towns of their respective countries to provide themselves with treatment and purification systems for waste. This is particularly interesting in that it would seem to indicate that in the tourist resorts in which the residents have a greater awareness and tourist culture, there is also a sense that a holiday resort cannot sink below certain crucial levels of environmental quality.

### 4.2.3 The evaluation of the natural environment

The situation of the natural environment as it appears today compared to twenty years ago would seem to be have worsened in almost all the resorts analysed. The condition of the natural environment is judged to have improved only in the towns in which the environment constitutes one of the principal attractions.

### Comments

In almost all the cases examined, the conditions of the environment have worsened or, in the oldest resorts, have remained more or less unchanged. In cases in which the environment constitutes a tourist attraction, and thus an economic asset to be saefguarded, there are certain regulatory mechanisms, previously absent, aimed at its exploitation for tourist purposes. In these cases, the environment has not suffered from building speculation, has not been spoilt and would seems to have developed a tourist industry which not only appears compatible with the environment but which actually tends to promote it.

### 4.3.1 Negative effects

- loss of the identity and the traditional culture of the local community;
    Due to the altering of the social structure and the traditional system of economic relations;

- disappearance of traditional occupations;

- limits to the professional opportunities due to the economic dominance of tourism;

- low motivation for professional approach;
    due to easy and rapid enrichment, at least in the early phases of the development of a resor, generally due more to profits from property or commercial positions rather than from the actual activity in the tourist trade.

- cultural subordination to the objectives of the tourist industry;

- subordnation to decision-makers external to the area;

- competition between residents and tourists over the purchase or rent of flats;

- immigration of marginal strata with illegal or semi-legal activities;

- problems of social security (crime)

### Comments

The negative effects increase with the level of tourism development and the more this has been aimed at a mass market. In traditional resorts which grew up in the nineteenth century, the social structutre has adapted itself to the tourism model. In these cases the local culture includes the tourist culture, or rather the tourist culture has become itself a constitutive characteristic of the tradition of the resort. On the other hand, in those resorts which have developed in recent years at the pace demanded by the high growth rate of the contemporary tourist industry, there have been rapid changes in socio-economic organisation and the residents and local authorities have found considerable difficulties in reconciling its traditions and practices with the growth of the new industry. The case of Corfu is a particularly striking example of this.

Investment and socio-economic changes occur more rapidly if they take place as a result of the intervention of non-local investors. Today, in fact, this would seem to be the case more often than not. In these cases, the local authority:
    - submits to the logic of economic development imported from outside;
    - is unable to control the direction of this development;
    - tends to allow decisions to depend on the choices of external investors.

In these conditions, it is difficult for the traditional professions and trades of an area to find a space of their own, although there are a few exceptions. On the other hand, land and buildings tend to increase in value, along with even simple activities such as the sale of staple goods. This can give rise to a sort of effortless enrichment (at least in the early stages of the development of a tourist resort) creating the illusion that growth and economic well-being can be enjoyed in the long term without a simultaneous development of specific professional expertise and quality upkeeping of the product.

Whenever the tourist industry develops in poor economic areas, it can tend to become the only important economic activity and discourage other productive activities and possible diversification.

Finally, in the thousands of activities involved in tourism, there is often considerable room for marginal labour. Due to its precarious position on the labour market, this marginal labour force can constitute a reserve for the development of illegal activities.

### 4.3.2 Positive effects

- rise in the disposable income of the residents;

- ample opportunities for work and business connected with tourism;

- contact with other cultures;

- improvement in cultural and educational standards.

### Comments

The positive effects are more marked when there is a local or regional authority capable of regulating the growth of the tourist industry. In the case of the development of public services, for example, the role played by the local authority is crucial.

It has been observed that in the more recently developed resorts (over the last 20 to 30 years) the disequilibria in the social environment appear to be more serious and more widespread. In these cases, an inefficient or unprepared local authority tends to be overcome by the number of problems that the process of economic and social transformation gives rise to, losing sight of certain key objectives which are extremely difficult to recuperate once tourism has become established.

The most important priorities are the provision of a system of public services which can cope with the sudden increases in population and the encouragement given to the development of local entrepreneurs to enter the tourist trade. The Costa Esmeralda in Sardinia can be seen as an example of the neglect of these two priorities. In this area, almost all entrepreneurial activity is owned by non-residents, while the local population is employed above all in activities which are upstream with regard to the tourist industry, in the construction sector in particular. As this sector depends entirely on investment in tourism, the result is that the local inhabitants gain from tourism only to the extent that the industry expands and undertakes new building projects (also eating up land, raising pollution levels etc.) while not gaining in any way from its day-to-day activity. It is nevertheless true that the inhabitants of tourist areas enjoy economic conditions that are normally above those of non-tourist areas nearby. They also have the chance of meeting, on a cultural as well as an economic level, a host of visitors from different countries.

Whether the resort is old or new, it is relatively easy to start up new businesses, even with only relatively modest capital reserves, or to get regular seasonal work and thus provide an important supplement to the family income. Higher levels of income and the seasonal nature of the tourist trade also entail the possibility of increasing the average level of schooling.

### 4.3.3 Evaluation of the evolution of the socio-economic environment

The current situation of the tourist resorts analysed in comparison with those twenty years ago show:
- an improvement in economic conditions;
- a decrease in consensus over social conditions and quality of life.

### Comments

The greater wealth of the residents caused by the development of tourism is something common to all the resorts.

As regards social conditions (quality of life) there are instead different evaluations, from which it can be concluded that economic welfare has not automatically brought social welfare. This evaluation is typical of mature societies and can be found particularly among the younger and better-educated members of society. As this contrast is not co-extensive with social groups with different economic interests but rather cuts across all the members of society, the identification of possible discriminating variables is problematic; beeing this division political in nature, it may lead to difficulties in addressing medium-term actions from a pure economic point of view (plans, regulations, subsidies, etc.).

### 4.4.1 Negative effects

• over-intensive urbanisation;

• uniformity/anonymity of the areas of greatest tourism;
> There are generally two possibilities: either the buildings use the architectural forms typical of an area in a standardised and impersonal manner (particularly in the case of structures for entertainment use) or they take on foreign models or exasperate local forms to the extent of becoming kitsch.

• overburdening the capacities of the resort;

• excessive traffic with respect to the main roads and available parking facilities;

• illegal buildings;

• degradation of the urban environment and decaying tourist structures due to low maintenance.
> This is not a generalised phenomenon but can be observed in the tourist resorts which undergo particularly severe crises in which there is high price competition with a consequent reduction of capital available for routine maintenance;

• aesthetic pollution
> This is due to a variety of factors: from the poor architectural quality of the buildings to the lack of regulations regarding commercial signs;

• noise pollution

### Comments

To summarise, many of the problems listed here can be traced to the high boost in the value of property in tourist resorts. The disequilibrium which arises between supply and demand in areas reserved for building or built-up land caused by the progressive increase in tourism gives rise to intensive exploitation of all areas that can be given over to use for tourism and in related services. The development of mass tourism, in particular, has resulted in a dramatic acceleration in urbanisation. In this case, nothing acts as the sort of brake on the exploitation of the environment that results from targeting high level demand (able to pay the price of better environmental quality). The growth of a mass tourism in an area is often accompanied by low quality in terms of the building undertaken for tourist use. Budget limitations and the size of the demand to be satisfied leads to the construction of highly standardised buildings, often of a low architectural style.

The overburdening of the capacity of a resort can result both from the structural limits of the original design of the resort or later from shifts towards new market segments requiring a different urban organisation. An example of this might be the week-end tourists that puts considerable stress nowadays on the traffic capacity of seaside resorts originally aimed at and planned for residential tourism.

### 4.4.2 Positive effects

- provision of public and private services above the average level of cities of the same size;

- concern for urban appearance;
    This can take various forms: concern for the collection of rubbish, for the equipment and infrastructure used by the inhabitants, etc.

- conservation and making the most of local architectural features/identities;

- retraining of decayed buildings and degradated urban areas.

### Comments

Tourist spending, added to that of the residents, leads to larger public and private services compared to those of urban centres of a similar size. Even in highly-seasonal tourist resorts, some part of the tourist services remains for the use of the residents in the seasons which have no tourist activity. Often it is the private rather than the public services which are over-abundant for the size of the area.

Apart from the resorts which put the environmental quality as a core factor of their development strategies, there is the evidence that only when the resorts enter the maturity stage of their life cycle - but never before -, greater attention is paid to the need to increase the quality of urban life. Also in these cases the need for interventions appears to be more instrumental to the reasons of the business than to the needs of the host population.

### 4.4.3 Evaluation of the evolution of the urban environment

Basically in the tourist destinations analysed, the quality of urban life is judged deteriorated compared with twenty years ago. The sole exceptions are those resorts which have seen the urban environment as a prime factor in competitivity.

In the older tourist centres, property development connected to the tourist trade came to an end some time ago, but despite this, judgments on urban quality remain negative. Other factors, in fact, lead to decreases in the quality of the city. Amongst these must be cited the diversification of the target demand of many resorts: new market segments towards which the tourist resorts have reoriented their demand often lead to the need to exploit environmental resources in unexpected ways, giving rise to stressful situations. An example which emerged from this research was the explosion of week-end tourism in resorts formerly oriented towards residential tourism, and which found themselves faced with traffic problems they are unable to cope with.

The changes in the environment as previously defined (natural, socio-cultural and urban) contribute to increasing or decreasing the competitivity of the tourist resorts.

From our research the following factors related to the environment are reported to have contributed to increase the competitivity:

- the utilisation, safeguarding and improvement of the areas with natural beauty;
- the improvement of communications and of transport networks;
- the realisation of tourist ports;
- the hospitality of the residents (often traditional in character);
- the existence of residential areas targeted at a high market;
- the safeguarding and improvement of the urban environment (gardens, flowers, cleanliness, revitalisation of the historic centre)
- the existence of an efficient reflux water purification system.

The following environmental-related factors are reported to have decreased competitivity in the seaside resorts:

- sea pollution
- algae and dead seaweed in the sea
- crime
- overcrowding
- noise pollution
- the degradation of the areas near the tourist resort
- the degradation of the countryside
- intensive building in the area
- bad quality of urban space

Comments

Not all the negative effects of tourism development on the environment, however it is defined, have correspondingly negative effects on the competitivity of the resort.

There are two reasons for this:
- some of the negative effects of tourist development are not noticed by visitors but only by residents;

- not only are some of the negative changes to the environment not noticed by tourists; for some segments they can even constitute an attraction.

The latter aspect is of particular importance in that research on the subject (cf. Chapter 5) would seem to show that there is a sort of adaptation of demand to the various levels of environmental quality of the different resorts. Certain declining resorts in terms of environment may not have a corresponding decline in terms of the share of the market. The target segment with a high degree of sensibility to environmental factors may simply be substituted for ones which have less sensibility. An important example of this is Rimini which, during the environmental catastrophe caused by the appearance of the algae, managed to penetrate segments of the tourist market which were substantially indifferent to this phenomenon and for whom the resort preserved quasi intact its attraction (week-end and congress market).

The list of interventions on the environment which improve the competitivity of a resort are a summary of the indications offered by the dossiers on the tourist resorts analysed. Two of these (the improvement of communications and transport networks and the realisation of tourist ports) have little to do with improving the quality of the environment but are rather to be seen as potential dangers to it. They have nevertheless not been eliminated from the list as they indicate well how competition on the tourist market still rests on factors such as accessibility or target diversification. Most of the actions undertaken for the defence of the environment are basically oriented towards improving the urban landscape, although the stronger and more determined ones are limited to a fairly small number of resorts.

Evaluations of the relation between tourism and environment in the various resorts have at least one aspect in common. While evaluations as to changes over the last 20 years in terms of the quality of the environment, (following our three definitions) are all negative or at best indicate no change, the only consistently positive evaluation was that relating to the growth in wealth of the residents in the areas in which tourism development took place. The exchange that has taken place is thus clear: local communities have put their area, their culture and their resources (human, capital, etc.) in the hands of the tourism industry in exchange for a general increase in income. This exchange took place in all resorts regardless of the model of tourism development followed.

The aspects that vary considerably from one resort to another (and thus from one model of tourism development to another) are instead the proportion of income produced by the tourist industry that remains with the residents and the prospects that the system has in terms of its capacity to continue to produce satisfactory levels of this income. In this sense, the survey highlights very different situations, ranging from:
1) full involvement of the local inhabitants in the tourist industry (supply and sales strategy), who in this case have direct control over the flow of demand;
2) involvement of the residents only as regards the management of the supply structures, with demand controlled by the tourist agents;
3) the involvement of most of the local population only in activities (building in particular) stemming from a developing tourism industry and not involved at all when the tourism system operates in a situation of stationary equilibrium.

From the point of view of the natural environment the latter case (pointed out in Costa Smeralda in Sardinia) gives rise to perhaps the most dangerous situation amongst those indicated, as the mechanism of production and distribution of wealth to residents acts only when the tourist industry develops quantitatively (more hotels, more holiday flats, etc.); when growth is blocked the income of the residents is reduced dramatically. The consumption of the natural environment thus becomes the necessary condition for the residents to enjoy the profits of tourism.

The opposite is true of Eastbourne (UK), where not only is the resident population involved in tourist activity, but there are no intermediaries in its relation with demand and there are strong incentives for maintaining not only the natural but also the urban environments intact. The tourist structure of this old resort, which grew up at the turn of the century, have become themselves a factor of attraction, and their maintenance is thus today one of the prime objectives of the local tourist agents.

The case of Eastbourne, compared to that of the Costa Smeralda or even more to that of Corfu, introduces the subject of "time" in the relations between tourism and environment.

• TIME
There are three distinct phases in which this variable influence these relations:

- at birth: the demand pattern for holiday dominating at the beginning of tourism in every resort characterize its supply structure in an almost indelible way even in subsequent years;

- in the long term: encouraging the assimilation of tourism culture into the original cultural models of the host population;

- in the short term: when cyclical fluctuations of tourist demand and the consequent economic results affect the attention to, desire for and financing available for interventions on the environment;

The second phase is perhaps the most important and also the least examined. In the older resorts, in fact, there is a tendency to integrate the forms of tourism "production" within the cultural models of the residents, so that the organised hospitality becomes an integral part of the culture of the inhabitants of the resort.

In all the resorts analysed, tourism development has brought about a break with pre-existing economic, social and cultural models. While in the older resorts this has taken place over a period of decades, in the more recent holiday centres it has happened much quicker, and the time available for assimilating the tourist culture on the part of the pre-existing local culture has been extremely short. This has led to particularly serious difficulties and imbalances in the approach and in the management of this "new" industry, with severe repercussions on the natural environment and on the social organization itself.

Other factors which appear to play a central role to define/analyze the status of the relationships between tourism and environment are:

• RESIDENT'S PARTICIPATION IN THE TOURISM PRODUCTION PROCESS
The level of control exercised by the residents within the tourism process (the management of the accommodation/leisure structures and also some degrees of freedom in the commercial strategy) allow for a greater autonomy in the management of the territory.
This autonomy can favourite processes of endogenous development which normally includes goals of reproduction (territorial, economical, generational) and, to certain extents, give raise to:
  • self limitations of the growth (basically due to the competition between internal and external operators);
  • product diversification and innovation;
  • forms of cooperation between local operators.

These effects are much less frequent in the cases where external operators (Tour Operators, hotel chains, airline companies, real estate companies) control the the management of the *filière touristique* (see also Debbage, 1990).

• SOCIAL AND ECONOMIC CONDITIONS
The social and economic base on which tourism development builds on is important to determine the relationships between local operators, host populations, external agents. Ad example pre-existent unsubordinated conditions (both economical and cultural), the presence of economic alternatives to tourism, give residents more negotiating powers with respect to

the promoters of tourism development. This means not only that the opportunities for tourism offered can be accepted or rejected, but above all that the forms and models of development can be influenced.

•THE ENVIRONMENT AS A DISTINCTIVE MARKETING FACTOR
An other factor affecting the relationships between tourism and environment is the role of the environment in the marketing of the resort (expecially promotion and communication). The more the environment (under the forms of natural areas, cultural and historical centers, qualification actions, ect.) is utilized as a distinctive factor by the marketing of the resort, the more becomes (is perceived as) an economic asset necessary to the re-production and thus to be safeguarded for tourist ends.

These elements will be returned to in the chapter 7.

# 5. PROMINENT ACTORS IN THE RELATIONSHIP BETWEEN TOURISM AND ENVIRONMENT

## 5.1. INTRODUCTION

One of the aims of the research was to identify and analyse the behaviour of the various actors involved in tourist activity towards the environment.

In fact the different outcomes of the relationship between tourism and the environment in the resorts analysed depend not only on the context-related macrovariables (cf. chapter 4.), but also on the role of the various entities involved in the hospitality industry and on their interactions.

The results of this research phase gave rise to an analytical description of the mechanisms, which in the various resorts observed, led to the present tourist organisation. This also forms the basic informative material to try to identify the key system of relationships between the different entities involved in the hospitality trade which defines the real tourism organisation in the resort.

Three main categories of actors emerge from the research:

- tourist operators of supply and demand;
- local government bodies;
- the local population and organised groups

which directly or indirectly influence the environmental asset in the resorts analysed. In each case these actors have specific features: the following paragraphs provide summaries of the three groups which do not include specific local references.

## DEMAND TOURIST OPERATORS

The Tourists (evidences from the case-history analysis)

Environmental problems are noticed by the tourists only when they affect the enjoyment of the "tourist product". An attitude of awareness towards the "environmental issue" is generally very rarely adopted when on the spot.

This evaluation is not astonishing: the tourist behaves like a consumer; he chooses a resort for its specific qualities and he feels ready to leave it if and when it falls short of his expectations.

Therefore, he does not adopt a constructive attitude towards any environmental problems, given that they only concern the tourist for the holiday period and not necessarily the following year when he chooses a different resort altogether, thus eliminating any problem in the first place.

Almost everywhere, the most felt problems concern vehicle traffic and parking congestion, noise from any source, dirt of any kind and visible pollution (both aesthetic and environmental). Of course, in the case of residents in second homes, the state of the building is also of importance. In a few cases, where the development has been controlled with difficulty, problems concerning the water supply and the lack of facilities are noted (especially in cases where there has been recent and rapid tourist development).

All the vehicle traffic restrictions are generally welcomed quite favourably, while the attempt to discourage the use of cars through high parking fees is not approved of.

However, it must be emphasized that in the resorts examined, no particularly binding restrictions were introduced. Therefore, it is difficult to estimate tourist reactions in any detail.

However, the consideration already made is important: it clearly appears that tourists do not favourably view all those conditions, even environmental ones, which make their stay uncomfortable. Therefore, we can assume that, generally speaking, restrictive policies aimed at improving environmental conditions (traffic, noise and environmental pollution) are welcomed.

A specific evaluation must be made for tourists attracted mainly by cheap prices. In fact, these are consumers oriented almost exclusively towards a quick deal, without paying any special attention to the resort where they are located. In the long run the emphasys on this type of tourists creates a homogenisation of offer and wipes out any special features the different resorts might have. The consequences are obvious: both the natural and cultural environments lose their identity and in this sense there is a loss of quality both for the holiday resort and the tourist.

## The Tour Operators

Like the tourists, the tour operators have a "precarious" nature towards the spot, in the sense that they can decide to leave the resort if the demand changes or the real profits are lower than expected.

As these companies are sometimes able to handle considerably large flows of tourist demand, they express organised and stable economic interests. Therefore, they intervene directly or indirectly to determine the quality and features of the supply structures to be carried out in the tourist resort which is the object of their business.

Their relationship with the environment is based on criteria of essentially short-term interest. In fact they:

- are mostly concerned and usually put pressure in delivering quality services inside the tourist structures but are rarely involved with the management of the external environment;

- do not make investments to protect the environment in the resort which they market; on the contrary their business imperative may lead them to environmental non-compatible objectives (i.e. maximizing the number of clients);

- if the consumer no longer likes the resort due to any problems of environmental deterioration they use not to intervene to support restoring the environmental quality, but shift the tourists to new destinations.

## SUPPLY TOURIST OPERATORS

Whereas on the tourist demand side, there are on the whole very few different types of entities, on the supply side there operate a lot of actors whose relationship with the environment varies according to a number of variables.

### • Hoteliers
As a category, no particular awareness of environmental problems was detected, but environmental awareness was noted at an individual level and is often welcomed as an opportunity to give rise to:

a) improvements in the quality of the supply;
b) cost decreasing;
c) entry into new market segments.

### • Operators of Leisure and Recreational activities
Leisure activities (theme parks, discothèques, etc.) generally build artifical environments as they have different characteristics from the place where they are set up. They only need to be easily accessible with good links to the transport network.

•Real estate agents
It's the economic category less environmental-sensible. The real estate activity is carried out by companies that are ready to welcome the opportunity of easier and quicker profit, without any view to long-term economic management. In these cases, the main interest lies in the use of the land without worrying about its consequences and the continuity of the tourist trade.
Their action can be bring less damage to the environment in 2 cases: when "controlled" (i.e. when they operate within strict building regulations) or, authonomously, when the location is adressed to demand of a high level: in these cases environmental values must be exploited in order to be able to successfully deal with this targets. The real estate agents operating in these areas of demand show particular awareness of the conservation of the natural environment in which they have placed their investments and even of the building methods used.

•Tourist operators who deal and make business with the environmental product of the resort: tourist guides, lifeguards, swimming clubs and sailing clubs, etc. These categories are interested in protecting the environment in so far as the resort already offers environmentally friendly tourist products.

Comments:

The environmental issue seen as a whole is rarely considered by the private operators. Their horizons and field of initiative remain limited to the area of ownership or at the most to the area in which their property is located.

A significant exception to this behaviour occurred on the Romagna coast at the time of the worrying dead seaweed problem. In the latter case, both the individual tourist operators and their associations developed a strong reaction to protect the environment, both through individual and group intitiatives. The cause of the reaction was the sudden and violent threat to the main point of tourist attraction: the sea. In other words, the very source of the tourist business was drammatically threatened.

It is easy to generalize this behaviour: whatever the size of their company, economic operators tend to adopt a strictly business attitude towards environmental problems. This attitude becomes general and polical with consequent individual and group actions (like entrepreneurial associations) when the threat to the environment becomes a threat to the very sources of business.

Generally speaking, the impact of these tourist entities depends on the efficiency of the local government and on its ability to establish rules for sensible town planning and make sure they are observed.

However, it must be stressed that the tendency to react to environmental damages is less marked under certain circumstances:

a) in new resorts, where there is a tendency to accept any method of tourist development and land consumption so as to yield an immediate profit;

b) in resorts addressed to tourist demands with primary low-spending goals, where the return on investment is low and the push towards an improvement of the environment is not supported from the tourists side;

c) in the resorts (usually long established) which nowadays bases their attractiveness on the" artificial" resources (leisure facilities, i.e. theme parks, discos, pubs, etc.) more than on environmental ones;

- Municipal Government:

  This body mainly deals with control of building activities, control of vehicle traffic, equipment of the resort with suitable public facilities (purification plants, transport, aqueducts, sewerage, etc). Sometimes play an important role at the municipal level the Environmental Department and the Town committees on environmental issues with advisory powers made up of environmental associations, farmers and trade associations.

- Supramunicipal Government:

  These bodies deal mostly with regional planning or environmental improvements and protection which cover particularly vast areas. Sometimes play an important role at the supramunicipal level an Intermunicipal consortium to help the municipalities to deal with land management, the Provincial level (provincial government departments for the environment and trade), the Regional level (regional government departments for agriculture, zootechny, fishing and public works).

Comments:

The main body in all cases is the municipal government.
The function that it is meant to perform is not always suitable for the problems caused by tourist development. It is this very inadequacy, found especially in the most recent resorts, which highlights the importance of municipal government in controlling the activities within its jurisdiction.

Although its actions does not have a direct and immediate effect on the competitiveness, it is one of the main elements that make it possible and lasting in time (i.e. the equipment of the resorts with suitable facilities has avoided serious damage to the environment).
In cases where the efficiency of governmental entities is greater, suitable municipal committees on environmental issues are set up (whose remit is to advise) formed by representatives of the production sectors and the most important environmental associations. These committees have the important task of voicing the interests weighing on the resort and allowing a public debate on the aims of development and solutions to environmental problems.

However, the existence of government or local authority departments with responsibility for the environment is not always a guarantee of efficiency, given that formal authority is not always matched by real powers.

In overcoming inefficiency at the municipal level the technical and planning support given by supramunicipal levels has been found useful: especially that of intermunicipal and provincial levels. However, these interventions and these organizational forms seem to be effective only when the municipal level remains efficient and autonomously decides whether to intervene or not.

Sometimes the controlling activity of the public actors is less efficient, because they are subject to the double pressure of the interests both of the investors and of local population which are basically the same at least in the first phase of tourism development. When this occurs there may be an absence of planning and government.

The decision of the government to relinquish their role can occur for various reasons:

1) cultural subordination to economic development reasons brought by the local populations (the electors in ultimate analysis) and large investors;

2) direct economic interest of the political class in areas with a socioeconomic growth which is too rapid and lacking in efficient government and administration traditions.

Often, there have been intervenctions by a supramunicipal authority (municipal, provincial and regional consortia, etc.) which deals with planning or intervenes on specific issues (public works, agriculture, etc.). However, these actions also have different effects: in the regions where public administration is relatively inefficient, these interventions are very slow and not very productive.

On the other hand, where public administration has a tradition of efficiency, they tend to be important and sometimes decisive. In fact, land exploitation and building speculation activities for tourist purposes tend to have homogenous and equal features in all the resorts; but there is less of an impact (sometimes much less) where the institutional bodies carry out efficient controls.

Very often, even in the regions with efficient administrations, the interventions are of a sectorial and uncoordinated nature and there is no involvement between the authority in charge of tourism and the authority in charge of the environmental policy.

## The Host Population

In the resorts analyzed the relationship between the resident population and tourists generally does not show problems, but it must be considered that the situations analyzed are tourist "machines" used to cope with numbers.

Some tensions arise only when the resort exceeds its capacity. However, the criticism is not aimed at the tourists, but to the supply system and in particular to the tourist operators: the tourists are not particularly held responsible. When the overcrowding becomes excessive and causes problems (traffic, pollution etc.) for the resident population, they tend to criticise the operators deemed responsible for such problems due to excessive greed and lack of attention.

Secondly, the local government is called into question due to the shortage of town facilities arranged as a result of a lack of programming of the tourist flows and the poor control made on the activities of the operators.

The research doesn't allow to confirm potential conflicts between the resident population involved in tourist activity and the resident population which is not involved.

Social control in tourist systems is not uniform and varies widely, expressing itself according to the forms prevailing in the resort area. For example, in Rimini the system of interpersonal relations (family ties, bonds of friendship and neighborliness) exercises strong social control on the operators and on the uninvolved population, thus preventing the outbreak of conflict.

Generally speaking, there is a tendency to maintain the status quo even when the environmental conditions have worsened. However, the bond of solidarity between populations involved and those uninvolved becomes critical when the usefulness of such a social alliance is lacking or threatened. In the specific case, this occurs when the difficulties arising from the tourist economic activities become much greater than the benefits received.

This tendency to maintain the status quo can be a positive factor if the environmental bug catches on: that is to say, when the main trend becomes protecting or improving the environment.

## Environmental Associations

Environmental associations actually come between the entities making up a part of the environment and the governmental bodies, since they are the political expression of the attention and problems of the population towards the environment.

There are environmental associations and groups active in every resort analyzed. In developed countries there may also be "green" political parties.

Sometimes, the associations and groups are local sections of national organizations.

Their purpose is always and above all to protect and preserve the flora, fauna and the land. In the areas where the environment is used to attract the tourist, there are groups and associations which try to spread environmentally friendly tourism. Sometimes in other resorts the associations offer proposals for the correct tourist use of the area: this is to prevent the tourist facilities from damaging any further a resort which is already overpopulated.

These environmentalist associations and groups make people aware of the environment and only sometimes manage to influence political decisions and the local population. They have less influence on the tourists and almost none at all on the economic operators.

A comparison was undertaken between two resorts which are very different in terms of tourist tradition, size and the role of the environment, and in particular the natural environment, in tourist product policies. It is important to bear this fact in mind when considering the results of this comparison.

Rimini is a traditional tourist resort (in 1993 it will celebrate 150 years of tourist activity) and is of considerable size (150,000 inhabitants). Its position in the tourism market is heavily based on social elements (hospitality, friendliness, congenial atmosphere) and on urban and artificial features (entertainment, fun, artificial parks) while the "pure" natural aspects are secondary in terms of the product appeal. Rimini sells comfort, entertainment and hospitality; the first two by means of continual reinvestment in the "artificial" environment, the third through a centuries-old custom of the local population of welcoming and satisfying the tourist in every way (to the extent that we can speak here of a spontaneous culture of hospitality).

L'Estartit is a relatively recent resort and is small in terms of its urban centre (5,000 inhabitants). It became a tourist resort around 40 years ago and was oriented towards the sun and beach segment. Its natural resources have now been turned into a strong point in terms of its position on the tourist market. The best example of this is its natural under-water park. L'Estartit's natural environment constitutes its main tourist attraction and distinctive characteristic. It is clear that in this case there is a greater awareness and care on the part of the local inhabitants and organisations towards the conservation of these easily identified natural resources, on which tourist activity depends.

| Major advantages perceived of tourism development | | |
|---|---|---|
| | Rimini | L'Estartit |
| - Increase in earnings | 91% | 59% |
| - Creation of new jobs | 89 | 68 |
| - Improvement of quality of life | 68 | 48 |
| - Development of services and infrastructure | 57 | 50 |
| - Traditions are being made the most of | 41 | 21 |
| - Conservation of the landscape | 16 | 20 |
| - None | 1 | 7 |

There is substantial agreement in terms of the ranking of the advantages that tourism brings even though the population of Rimini is more favourable toward tourism than those of L'Estartit.

The **economic advantages** (income and improved work opportunities) are the most obvious advantages, even if the proportion of people who declare this to be an advantage in L'Estartit is much lower than that of Rimini. In the latter, the perception of this type of advantage is entirely transversal, that is, it is shared by people of both sexes and different ages, professions and economic positions in the tourist sector.

Opinions are much more sharply divided in terms of improvement in the **quality of life**, both within the resort and between the two resorts (less than half the sample in the Spanish resort indicated it as an advantage). In general, young people tended to express a more favourable opinion than the older generation, as did those directly involved in tourist activity.

It is interesting that in both resorts the **development of services and infrastructures** is seen to be an advantage to a much greater extent by families with children than those without.

Comments

The advantages perceived by tourism development are mainly tied to economic welfare and to job opportunities. These benefits are on the whole shared by many different layers of population, even by those not directly involved in tourist activity.

| Major disadvantages perceived of tourism development | Rimini | L'Estartit |
|---|---|---|
| - Increase disorder, life more difficult | 76% | 37% |
| - Irregular growth of the city | 65 | 58 |
| - Risk of spoiling the landscape | 50 | 67 |
| - Fewer economic alternatives, tourism-dependence | 45 | 44 |
| - Generation of social tensions | 34 | 27 |
| - Threat to local culture and traditions | 23 | 27 |
| - Local people less independent in their choices | 20 | 25 |
| - None | 9 | 3 |

In the analysis of the disadvantages, sharper differences emerge between the two resorts, probably linked to the different emphasis of each on the environment.

For the inhabitants of Rimini, the disadvantages of tourism are those linked to the **overcrowding** which puts the social environment under pressure, as well as to the uncontrolled growth of structures and infrastructures which affect the urban environment. For the inhabitants of Escartit, on the other hand, the risks concerning the degradation of natural resources are dominant.

**Risk of spoiling the landscape**: there would seem to be a higher sensitivity towards this factor amongst young people and those with a higher level of education.

**Threat to local culture**: indicated particularly by **families**, almost as if it was a signal of a potential risk of not being able to transmit the typical values of one generation to the next.

It should be pointed out that in Rimini the section of the population not involved in tourism expresses more negative views than those who are dependent on it in terms of almost all aspects; whereas in the Spanish resort the opposite is true: those who are economically dependent on tourism are the ones which stress the disadvantages most.

In both resorts, those who tend to highlight the least the disadvantages deriving from tourism development are:
- the elderly
- those with a low level of education
- the non-workers

Comments

For the local population, the environment would seem to coincide with whatever brings profits and makes tourist activity possible. The disadvantages identified as being due to tourism seem to be above all those which put the future of the tourist economy itself at risk. There are no clear objectives in terms of the environment <u>per se</u> and for the exclusive use of the residents rather than as part of its possible exploitation at the level of tourism.

If this hypothesis should be confirmed, it would mean that awareness and care of environmental resources are possible only when they are functional to the satisfaction of tourism demand, either because they constitute the principal feature of attraction or because they are an important corollary of the tourist demand target.

They would seem nevertheless to be factors that operate above and beyond the hospitality culture: the perception of tourism development as a potentially problematic factor is identified above all by the younger and better-educated sections of the population.

The economic dependence or independence of the residents on tourist activity leads to evaluations that differ only slightly. In fact, this distinction would appear not to be of particular relevance here. These results would appear to preclude any strong pressure on the part of the population not involved in the tourist industry towards changes that would make the resort more environment-friendly.

Awareness of the possibility of tourism development compatible with environmental needs would thus seem to depend more on generational or cultural factors than on those of economic convenience. In this sense, those most in favour of intervention and action on environmental issues are the younger generation and those with a reasonably high level of culture and education, often with children, regardless of whether they are involved in the tourist sector.

All in all do you think the present environmental conditions of the resort are better or worse compared to the past?

|  | Rimini | L'Estartit |
|---|---|---|
| - Much better | 1% | 12% |
| - A little better | 34 | 30 |
| - More or less the same | 28 | 14 |
| - A little worse | 30 | 22 |
| - Much worse | 8 | 22 |

In both resorts, there is a general tendency to consider the present environmental conditions as slightly worse than those of the past. However, in both cases it is a discriminating factor as the local population is decisively split between optimists and pessimists.

Those who tend to be <u>optimist</u> (better conditions now than in the past) are in Rimini:
- the elderly
- those with a low level of education
- non-professionals.

and in L'Estartit:
- younger people (up to 35)
- those dependent on tourism to some extent for their income.

Those who tend to be <u>pessimist</u> (worse conditions now than in the past) are in Rimini:
- the central age group (36-59)
- those with high levels of education

and in L'Estartit:
- older members of society (over 60)
- those with children
- those economically independent of tourism

## Comments

The results confirm a potentially higher awareness of environmental issues amongst the younger members of society, amongst those with a higher cultural or educational background, and amongst those with children (with ideals for the future generations). The partial contradictions noted in L'Estartit (optimistic young people) can probably be interpreted as positive reactions to the recent interventions aimed at improving the natural resources of the area (the setting up of a under-water park, the safeguarding of other natural areas etc.).

## 5.5.4. Interventions Considered to be Important for the Improvement of the Area

Which of the following initiatives are felt to be definitely necessary to requalify the area ?- (multi response)

|  | Rimini | L'Estartit |
|---|---|---|
| - Limitation of private car traffic | 20% | 13% |
| - Improvement of transport service | 33 | 67 |
| - Improvement of surveillance | 94 | 58 |
| - More entertainments | 6 | 37 |
| - More attention to local culture | 35 | 40 |
| - Safeguard of landscape | 28 | 55 |
| - Improvement of infrastructure | 64 | 49 |
| - Noise reduction | 59 | 69 |
| - Air pollution reduction | 28 | 46 |
| - Water pollution reduction | 67 | 73 |
| - Limitation. of tourist flow | 16 | 25 |
| - Improv. in quality of tourism services | 33 | 32 |
| - Creation of green areas | 27 | 25 |
| - Waste control | 30 | 34 |
| - Promotion of the hinterland | 17 | 17 |
| - Other | 5 | 2 |
| - None | 1 | 1 |

The interventions considered to be of primary importance were:

- social control (surveillance), reduction of sea pollution and improvement of infrastructure (Rimini)

- reduction of sea pollution, noise pollution and creation of an efficient public service system service (L'Estartit)

Priorities in terms of interventions differ little in the two resorts. There is confirmation of a greater attention to factors regarding the natural and cultural environment in L'Estartit, probably due to the fact that these are the products that the resort sells at present. It is worth noting, however, the priority given to interventions aimed at improving the public transport system, reducing noise and increasing public safety. In Rimini, the latter is the most important factor. The control of the social environment and the improvement of the urban and artificial one constitute the urgent interventions, but they are also the ones most in line with the overall nature of the resort. Confirmation of this hypothesis can be seen in the priority given to the safeguarding of the landscape: less than 30% in Rimini and over 54% in L'Estartit. The reduction or control of sea pollution expressed by those in Rimini, if this hypothesis is valid, might have been the result solely of the fear of a tourist-repellent factor and not a moral imperative.

## Comments

In the analysis of the interventions necessary for the improvement of the resorts we can also see a movement towards those actions that are inspired by and tied to factors of tourism development. On the other hand, they could be explained by an excess of realism on the part of those (the population of Rimini) who cannot plead the cause of a natural environment that more or less no longer exists, and a quite obvious desire to conserve the natural environment where it is still in a good condition (L'Estartit).

We take the pragmatic position. Tourism development spreads benefits to wide sections of the population wherever it arises. Even if an individual is not directly involved, the beneficiaries will be members of the family or friends. In any case, the individual will be part of a general increase in living standards. This is sufficient to change the "genetic code" of the resident population, to infect it with the virus of the defence of social and economic interests, which tend to be identified with the dominant interest.

From this point of view, the resident population, even if it does not participate directly in the economic benefits of tourism, would seem to be in agreement with the rest of the population. Probably only in the case of very advanced degradation, when its interests are directly affected, would the residential population become a potential supporter of environmental improvement. As a preventive element, on the other hand, environmental improvement would seem to be of very little importance.

Having described the tourist entities operating in a tourist resort, an attempt can now be made to give a general picture of what happens, or can happen, to the environmental factors in a seaside tourist resort starting with the interactions between the actors.

The municipality is by far the most important of the institutional actors. Its position, for the purposes of this discussion, is crucial.

On the one hand, it is located in the lower band of government and on the other, it has powers and duties to represent the interests affecting the area: interests in development (also tourist) and interests in limiting the development itself.

It receives input from central and regional governments, generally because it has to govern the town, but sometimes also because it uses the funds for environmental development and improvement.

Generally speaking, both the central and regional governments do not have any direct influence on the resort.

However, it has been observed that while the central government has limited involvement (generally only for national legislation), the regional government (or provincial in a few cases) although not having any responsibility for direct intervention, does play an important role in controlling town planning. It is a good idea to stress this point, because it will form part of the final recommendations.

The regional level can actually in a few cases form a more balanced level of control, because it is less susceptible to pressure from local communities.

However, where there are particularly strong interests, not even the regional level is enough of a barrier.

In the following outline (see the pages below) this aspect of the problem has been highlighted through the illustration of "pressure" flows (both on the region and on the state) generally from the local population (for political elections) and from private organized groups (environmentalists, real estate businesses, etc) for lobby activities.

Other institutional levels may also be involved; for example consortia or associations between municipalities which have to provide technical service and assistance to the municipal governments (these services are normally in favour of several municipalities).

They can be considered important "support" levels, but not actually decision-making levels; therefore, they are not highly influenced by any lobby or pressure activities. However, the latter assume great importance in the case of municipal governments.

It is quite clear (though not surprising) that the municipal governments lack the suitable independence to make their own decisions as regards the local system they represent.

Therefore, they find themselves forced to deal with environmental problems in long established resorts, while they support expansion projects, within the limits of their jurisdiction, in resorts which are undergoing further development.

For this reason, we feel the only way to describe the interaction within the local resort is by giving all the actors, whatever part they might play, (from the local population to the real estate interests) the opportunity to air their views.

We have said that one of the most important tasks is to control town planning. In this sense, the immediate and direct interaction is with the real estate interests.

It is difficult for a municipal government to find the strength and political legitimation to come between obstacles or to object to individual investment aims in the case of resorts with expansive capacity and where the local population is not particularly motivated towards limiting the speed of development.

This is particulary true when the reasons for building development are supported by local entrepreneurs upon suggestions offered by external investors (whether they be tour operators or purely real estate agents), in this case the risk of not being able to make use of the "opportunities" for economic development (against the threat of choosing a different geographic location) makes it very difficult for all the local actors to make decisions. It is quite logical that in these cases few resorts will decide to decline promises of fast tourist development, which the actors involved consider a quick way to wealth.

Real estate investors (assuming that they are distinct actors) may find conflict in the case of the already sufficiently developed hotel sector, because the countering interests may counterbalance those in favour.
In this case, the municipal government finds itself in the position of having to choose between opposing interests: the more the resort is developed, the greater the pressure to prevent any further building expansion will be. In extreme cases, we may find ourselves faced with continuous and moderate building contractors orientated towards renovation and restoration activities.

In the more balanced situation, the orientations of those entities that are able to control the tourist demand will be of particular importance. That is to say, the possibility of entry into the market and of being able to control the incoming flows assumes particular importance. Therefore, building/real estate interests and hotel interests appear to be in a position of mutual control/balance, in the sense that a strong hotel sector is a sign of a long established resort and is also able to voice its opinions on the market as regards political decisions on expansion or town planning restrictions. Finally, additional activity may be performed regarding private or public entities by particularly important tour operators.

A separate word must be said about the leisure and business activities. Their interest simply lies in increasing the incoming flow and in this sense it seems impossible for them to voice their desire to veto building expansion (maybe quite the contrary).

They are more likely to create problems (even for the municipal government) regarding vehicle traffic, not so much to control or restrict it (unless the restriction does not positively affect the flow) as rather to develop its infrastructures (therefore, carparks, access roads, means of public transport etc).

It is actually due to this latter consideration that it is important to have a certain number of leisure activities with a low environmental impact, at worst, leisure activities which have a direct interest in preventing the natural resources from being used up beyond a certain limit.

This is the case of activities which exploit environmental resources of a certain area and which could find themselves in the position of having to decide to restrict their development, so as to make sure that the natural resource will remain intact in the future or in any case undamaged beyond a certain limit.

In cases of this kind, there is room for special local agencies that mostly represent the municipal government and private interests. They act as mediators and are responsible for guaranteeing that the behaviour of all the entities concerned is consistent with an undamaged environment.
In this sense, these agencies are different from environmentalist groups. The latter normally start as private non-profit organizations to carry on an activity of environmental awareness.

The service agencies, on the other hand, are established as instrumental entities with a view to intervening to actually guarantee a profit, otherwise ceasing due to damage to the main economic resource: the environment.

However, it is a good idea to repeat the fact that the establishment of this type of service agency is not the solution to environmental problems.

These assume importance when they are established following a debate (within the resort) involving all the economically and politically important entities and which leads to the precise conclusion that it is wiser (and more convenient) to invest in order to preserve than to build (this can be the case of a long established resort or a resort which is located in specifically environmental market areas).

The environmentalist groups in all the resorts with or without connections of a national nature mostly voice the issues put forward by opinion groups and as such put pressure on all the important entities. However, they do not have any particular influence except in sporadic cases.
Separate mention should be made of the local population:

It is difficult to give an exhaustive evaluation of an entity that is so difficult to describe in general terms. However, we can say that while on the one hand it takes part in the normal activity of requesting adequate facilities, for instance, vehicle order, etc., on the other hand, it is well aware of the direct and indirect economical advantages the tourist hospitality trade has.

Therefore, intollerance can only be slightly detected. On the contrary, in almost all cases, the population puts up with the burden of overcrowding (which moreover has become concentrated in the space of a few months) for the above-mentioned reasons.

The tourists are not permanent actors in a resort and must be classified according to the interest which brings them to a certain holiday resort.

Of course, their interaction is very frequently with the tourist structures.

However, where tourism is more permanent (generally second homes or elderly people who tend to stay for longer periods), prolonged interaction may be found with the local population or even with the government (usually to protest about any proposals for altering the resort).

In the proposed schemas, we have chosen to distinguish the flows offered as a guide and the relationship flows according to their qualities.
As is usual in these cases, we have decided to portay the type of existing relationship so as to avoid giving general importance to extreme cases.

Therefore, we suggest that attention be paid to the type of relationship as well as to the individual entities involved. In this way, several "relationship dimensions" can be noticed within the outline, each one having its own characteristics and qualities.

Therefore, the intersystemic relationships refer to systems that interact as a whole. The intergovernmental or service ones refer to relationships between public administration bodies or between special agencies and private operators. The lobby relationships refer to activities aimed at persuading other entities to make certain decisions, those of the market (with exchange and/or conflict procedures) refer to relations in which the entities, equipped with independent resources, can decide to exchange them, providing a mutual benefit, or purchase more of them at other entities' expense.

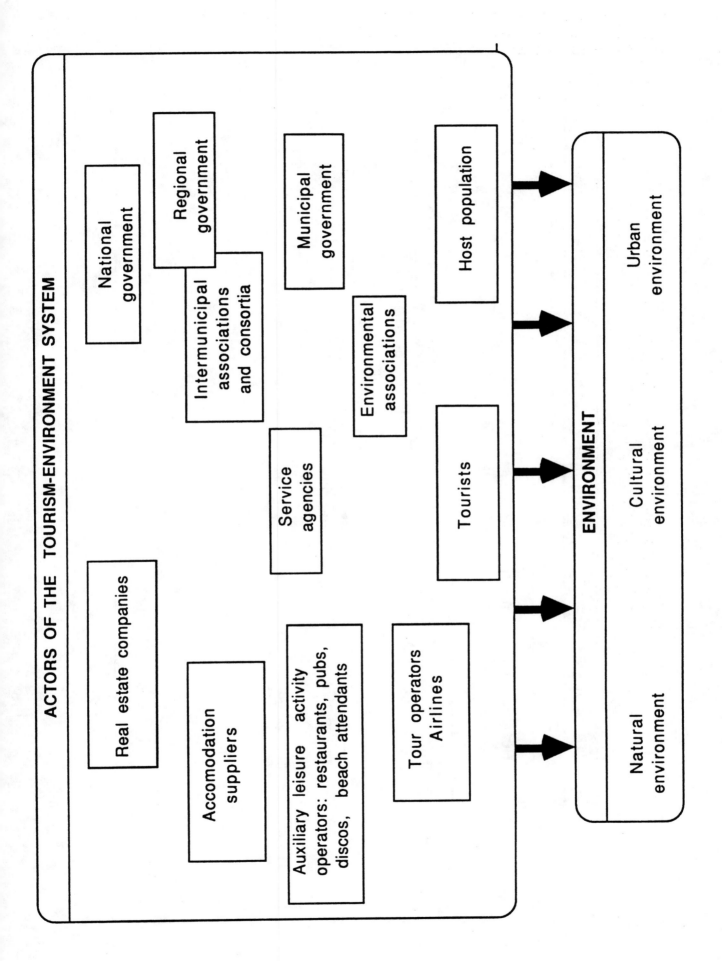

ACTORS OF THE TOURISM-ENVIRONMENT SYSTEM

National government

Regional government

Intermunicipal associations and consortia

Municipal government

Real estate companies

Accomodation suppliers

Service agencies

Environmental associations

Host population

Auxiliary leisure activity operators: restaurants, pubs, discos, beach attendants

Tour operators Airlines

Tourists

ENVIRONMENT

Natural environment

Cultural environment

Urban environment

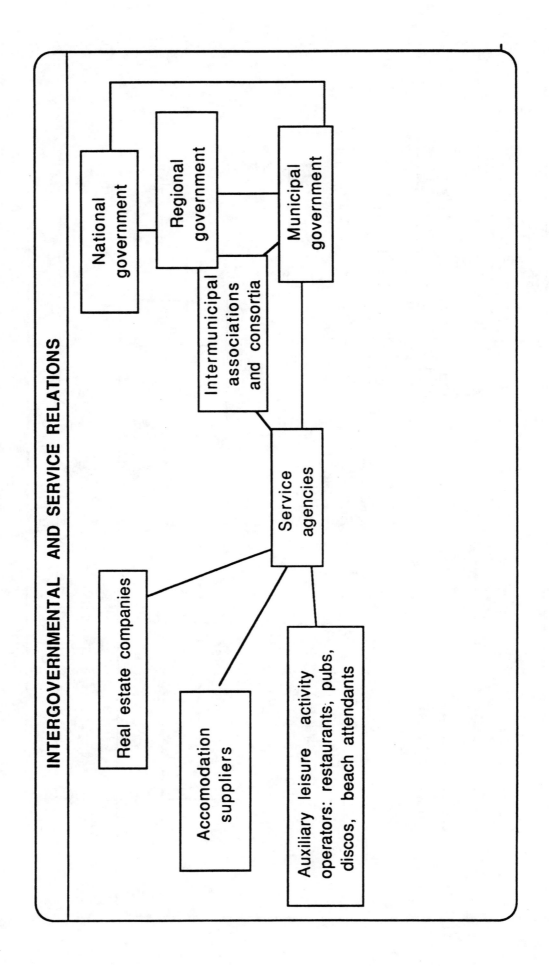

INTERGOVERNMENTAL AND SERVICE RELATIONS

National government

Regional government

Municipal government

Intermunicipal associations and consortia

Service agencies

Real estate companies

Accomodation suppliers

Auxiliary leisure activity operators: restaurants; pubs, discos, beach attendants

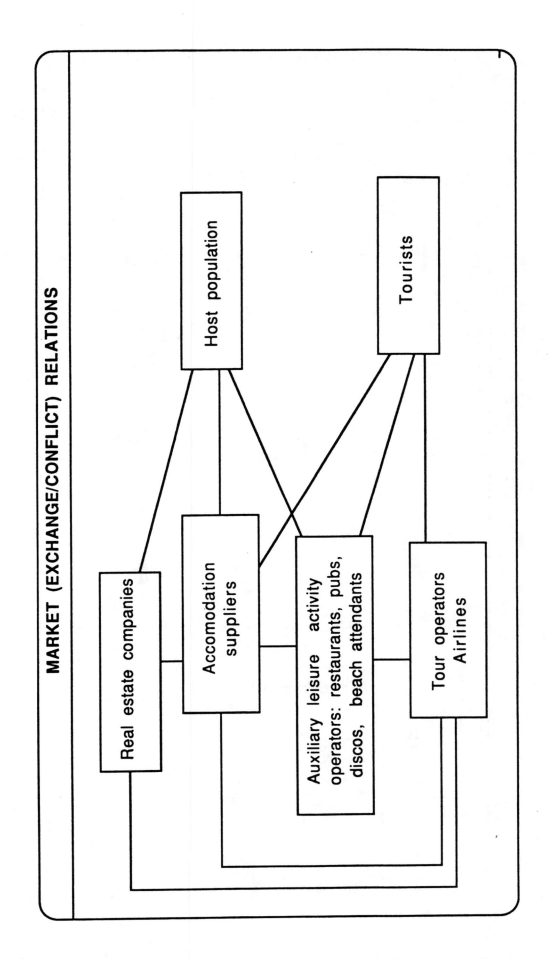

MARKET (EXCHANGE/CONFLICT) RELATIONS

Host population

Tourists

Real estate companies

Accomodation suppliers

Auxiliary leisure activity operators: restaurants, pubs, discos, beach attendants

Tour operators Airlines

# LOBBY RELATIONSHIPS

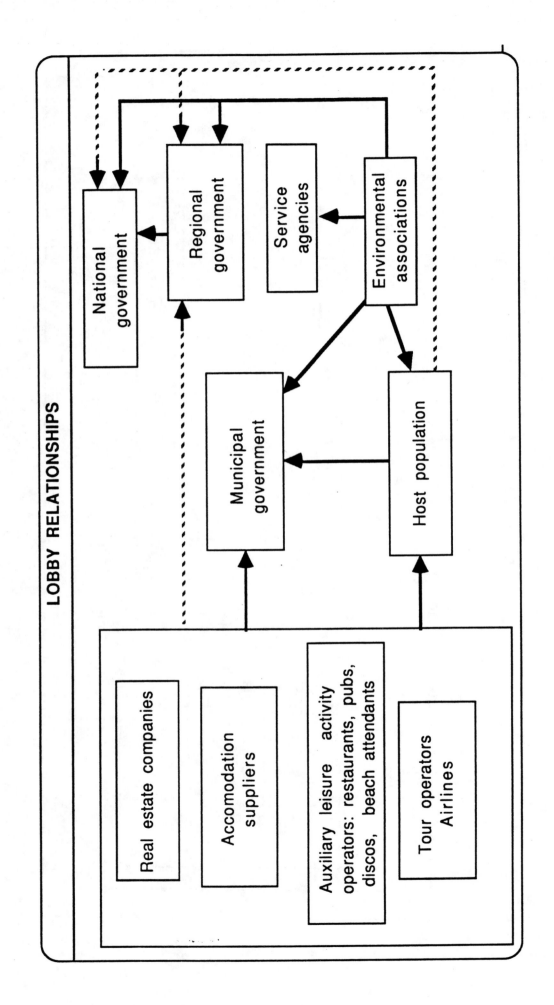

It is also possible to examine each individual relationship network by refering to each type of environment separately:

### 5.7.1. The Urban Environment
The type of relationship between private and public actors basically remains the same (usually lobby action) as does the intergovernmental type.

However, as regards the type of intervention on the environment, there is a series of decisive factors which each play a different role.

Generally speaking, the municipal government intervenes directly (usually public facilities) and through the passing of laws.

The central and regional governments (by carrying out control activities), the consortia between municipalities (through support activities) and the service agencies (by carrying out studies and putting forward proposals) also intervene through the municipal government.

The local population, business and leisure activities, building contractors, real estate agents and tourist activities directly intervene, even though they have to have special permission.

The tourists intervene directly, sometimes by imposing restrictions (for example, vehicle traffic).

Environmental groups intervene indirectly through lobby activity on the local population, on the tourists and on public administrations in general.

There is no doubt that the most important relationship is that represented by the four elements: economic activities in general (obviously, first of all the real estate and tourist activities), the tourists, the resident population and the municipal government. This relationship is delicate, because it represents the very heart of the urban problem.

### 5.7.2. The Natural Environment
In the case of the natural environment, while intergovernmental relationships remain quite stable, the powers of intervention of the regional and central public administrations show a considerable increase.

The flow of private entities, their relationship with the public administrations and the possibility of their intervening as regards the environment also basically remain stable.

### 5.7.3. The Cultural Environment

The cultural environment is quite a delicate matter, since it refers to aspects that cannot be measured in terms of quantity and, although having a wide meaning, it might include all that has been said up to now in describing the individual resorts.

However, due to the fact that we have to limit our illustration to the effects that tourist development has on the local community, we can only consider the most important relationship flows.

Due to the type of relationship that is established, we would tend to describe them all as potentially equal and conflicting, while granting a different title only to the tour operators.

This choice requires an explanation. All the entities within the resort undergo stress caused by changes, what we mean is that it is usually difficult to identify an entity or a category that manages to control all the variables of tourist development.

Moreover, where the local community does not control incoming flows, in fact, it submits to the control of demand carried out by external entities. It is clear that very often the same tour operators are subjected to the cyclic market trends, which are not controlled by them, and are dependent on macroeconomic variables.

However, even in these cases, the tour operators are considered demand controllers and therefore, in the eyes of the local operators, they usually adopt this role. So, for all these reasons, we are also persuaded to classify the tour operators as entities that can have a direct influence on the cultural environment of a resort where they manage flows of tourist traffic.

However, a distinction must be made within the resort: that between the population involved and the population uninvolved in the tourist sector.

In fact, while the uninvolved population tends to have a passive role, the involved population can only have the more active part in modifying tastes, trends, fashions, customs, etc., as well as undergoing greater changes itself.

In this way, a distinction is made between the population that is economically involved in the tourist sector (economic operators, involved population), the uninvolved population and local government (this does not have any special distinctions), whose task is to control and balance the two opposing trends (conservation/change).

# 6. ENVIRONMENT AND COMPETITIVENESS

In this chapter we briefly analyse both the type of interventions locally undertaken in favour of the environment and the projects that are meant to increase or regain the competitiveness of the resort analized in the tourist market.

The distinction between environment-oriented initiatives and tourist-related ones is sometimes not so evident because there is a wide area of overlapping between the two. Anyway not all initiatives in favour of the environment help the tourism relaunching (some are in fact are mainly devoted to resident population) as well as not all initiatives aimed at increasing the competitiveness of a resort have a positive impact on the environment.

It is our goal to verify whether the two areas can overlap, in other words whether the relaunching of a tourist resort comes as a consequence of the improvement of the environment or rather whether the environment is still an ancillary resource that can at the most benefit from a strategy that is aimed only at increasing the tourist flow.

## 6.1. ACTIONS IN FAVOUR OF THE ENVIRONMENT

The figure shows the results of our survey: the bigger the dots, the more frequently that intervention has been undertaken. Take into account that some situations are not easily comparable because in many cases the specific intervention is only occasional, while in other cases the action has a strategic value.

Comments:
Among the most common measures there is the *obligatory assessment of environmental impact* both for private and for public projects. In many cases such analysis is done by the private company that has promoted the initiative in order to prove its feasibility. It becomes therefore a crucial point that public administrations have the personnel qualified from a technical point of view to evaluate the projects and to approve of only those projects that are compatible with local resources.

Some of the most frequent initiatives are *excursions and other activities introducing tourists to nature* and to the discovery of the hinterland. However these activities are done on a regular basis, to the point that they involve the school system (L'Estartit), only in those areas where the environment has become the focus of the tourist business strategy.

Other initiatives,undertaken less frequently, involve themes aimed at improving the quality of the urban environment, such like:

- the development of green areas
- the creation of traffic-free zones
- the disposal of garbage
- the restoration of degraded buildings

• the control of air and noise pollution

The above measures are slowly entering current intervention policies in tourist areas; what is surprising is that this kind of intervention are not done in all the resorts analize, as a systematic improve to local quality of life.

Among the less frequent actions we find the following:

- *cooperation between operators in order to carry out environmental oriented initiatives*

- *restrictions to control the stream of visitors*

- *the development of environment-oriented strategies in the tourist development and promotion*

The three aspects we just mentioned give us useful hints to plan further actions.

1) cooperation between operators and common interventions are very important strategies to face the environment issue. Without proper action and cooperation between public Institutions and private business (with the goal of profit) the risk of having fragmentary initiatives and of missing effective results becomes very high.

As we have already seen the cooperation can be at different levels on the territory:
- portions of the municipal territory (environmental-homogeneous areas, neighbourhoods, etc.)
- the entire municipal territory
- areas bigger than the single municipality (partnerships of municipalities, regions, system-areas)

and involving various public and private actors, inside and outside the area, such as:
- different governmental departments of the given territory (municipal, regional)
- economic subjects operating in the area (site operators: accomodation and related facilities)
- operators who bring in the demand (TOs, airlines)
- economic operators not involved in the tourist business
- resident population and environment groups

2) Many resort areas among those analysed by the survey have established restrictions to the accomodation capacity of hotels and other accomodations. This measure can be of primary importance but is not enough. A seaside resort is rich in facilities and amenities for the entertainement, the amusement and the free time; this makes it extremely appealing to the one-day visitors (during the week-end also in the off-season).
The impact of these streams of visitors on the environment is often disruptive and yet restricting and managing them is not easy. Measures of de-marketing are not effective and besides they raise strong hostility on the side

of all those operators who benefit from these visitors (i.e. discoteque and amusement parks owners, etc.)

3) The developmentof an environmental-oriented concept in the development plannning and promotion of a given resort is very important. We can look at it this way: to a certain extent the profit can help improve the situation when the ethical principles are not enough. Turning the environment from a static resource into a factor of competitiveness means involving also all private operators in its protection and improvement: many people becomes aware that this makes their business successful and lasting, and that is especially true if they have experienced in the past the weakness of the environment-consuming development model.

This attitude is not free of risks: business activities tend, according to their own nature, to maximize the result of the activity and this has always been strictly related to the number of tourists, leading to an unbalanced situation.

Today we can overcome this contradiction: the market shows a demand of different needs, of individual behaviours and a demand for quality (and also, to a certain extent, the willingness to pay for the quality required). In the area of tourism environmental issues are the most important among the quality factors of a resort and will in the long term prevail on other factors tied to the services.

There are then the conditions so that the economic return the tourist operators are looking for will more likely come from the selection of targets willing to pay for the quality of the environment rather than from the maximum number of visitors tout-court.

On this idea could be based that solidarity between the environment and the economic operators that is in theory the only possible base for a compatible development.

The following charts show projects undertaken or in a well-advanced discussion phase that have the aim of relaunching areas onto the tourist market.

Observations

It is rather evident that each resort has much <u>inertia</u> in the development model that it permits the prevailing model (successful in the past) to continue its reproduction.

Two significant type cases are worth noting:

1) those resorts in which the environment has become an economic distinctive factor per se, an economic opportunity. In these cases the strategies for regaining competitiveness have a strong environmental value. The action is aimed not only at the market but also at the local population, including those attending schools and also those tourists already present: thus the environment has become culturally important.

2) those resorts that have experimented with intensive development models (highly environmental-consuming) and that today sell services rather than environment. In these cases the intervention strategy is direct to confirming the tourist development whilst the environmental recuperation is a by-product: in reality for these resort plans of recovery according to a more environmentally friendly model would have enormous costs.

Referring to this second type of resort a paradox arises: the necessity to improve the environment to regain competitiveness and the necessity to intensify the old model (non environmental friendly) to find the financial resources needed to do it.

The vicious circle is not apparent:

• an external (public) intervention exclusively aimed at the environment would require huge financial availability not to mention an efficient base on which to continue the action in a context where predisposition towards the plan would be short coming from the outset.

• an endogenous process that inserts into the traditional model elements of change toward environmental context is possible only when economic prospects exist that can still attract private and public capital.

Regarding the above interesting outcomes can be observed from the case of Rimini: the success of diversification which has transformed the resort from that of a traditional marine resort to that of an important congress centre at national level, has brought about a process of improvements (above all in the urban context) financed privately to render more coherent the product with the needs and the lifestyle of the new clientele.

Obviously this example cannot be a model for every resort. Therefore the success of the challenge lies in the capacity of:

1) preventing and supporting policies before the system arrives at the point of no-return from the vicious circle;

2) making the still profitable parts of the tourism local system finance the diversification of services in the direction of satisfying the demand for a better quality of the environment so starting a step-by-step approach toward a model of "softer" tourism.

| PROJECTS | ACTORS RESPON./FINAN. | INFLUENCES ON COMPETITIVENESS | POSITIVE EFFECTS ON THE ENVIRONMENT |
|---|---|---|---|
| **RIMINI (I)** Master plan for the complete re-organization of the beach and the neighbouring area | Public-private venture | Qualification of the beach services<br><br>Increase of facilities for recreation/leisure<br><br>Increase of the tourist season | Re-modellization of the beach by adding natural elements (downs)<br><br>Improvement of the urban environment and of the aesthetic of the landscape<br><br>**Note: hardly opposed by environmentalists** |
| Tourist harbour | Private operators | Diversification of the demand (nautical tourism)<br><br>New opportunities for business<br><br>Recovery of a rundown area | Recovery of a rundown urban area<br><br>**Note: opposed by residents** |
| Reuse of a historic building originally devoted to social tourism (colonie) for the creation of a service centre and multimedial facilities | Private operators | New facilities for congress/meetings/incentives<br><br>Increase the facilities and the services for entertainment open all year | Recovery of a deteriorated building<br><br>**Note: opposed by residents** |
| New theme park dedicated to sport, fitness and body care | Private operators | Diversification of the demand<br><br>Increase the facilities and the services for entertainment | None |
| Enlargment of existing theme parks | Private operators | Increase the facilities and the services for entertainment | None |

| EASTBOURNE (UK) | | |
|---|---|---|
| Tourist harbour (2 marinas) +apartments+hotels | Private operators | More water-based facilities Reconversion of a marshy area Qualification of the resort image **Note: opposed by environmental groups** |
| Eastbourne Park: a multi-purpose service centre: ricreation, leisure, education facilities in a natural area. The location is strategic for flooding control | Public-private venture | Increase the opportunities for attractions (sport, leisure, cultura, etc) Improve drainage and prevent possible future flooding |
| Requalification of the Downs area in a naturalistic way by means of: • car parking spaces relocation • re-introduction of original flora • information/education centre for the downland habitat and wild life • coastline centre • low cost accommodation for visitors • family-based catering facilities | Public-private venture | More opportunities to visit the area Re-introduction of original flora Extension to school tourism Visitors introduction to nature Improvement of natural habitat Decrease tourist congestion by making a wider area available for visitors **Note: opposed by civic committies who are afraid of greater number of visitor** |
| Tourist signposting scheme | Public organizations | Improve the effectiveness of stay Improve urban aesthetic |
| Renewal programme of a shopping street | Public-private venture | More and better shopping opportunities Requalification of urban environment |

| Project | Actor | Objectives | Environmental aspects |
|---|---|---|---|
| Permanent marketing action | Public organizations | Attract more tourists and maintain the resort as an attractive place<br>Improve the quality service through training<br>Encourage local firms to trade and connect among themselves | None |
| **LLORET DE MAR (E)** Tourist harbour | Private operators | Diversify tourist demand (nautical tourism)<br>Increase and improve supply services | None<br>**Note: hardly opposed by environmental groups** |
| Preservation and qualification of historical gardens | Public organizations | Tourist fruition of a green area | Preservation of a green area |
| Renewal of a urban square by creating a commercial/leisure area | Public organizations | More and better shopping and leisure facilities | None |
| Congress centre | Public organizations | Increase off-season demand<br>Diversify the tourist demand | None |
| Golf centre | Private operators | Diversify the tourist demand<br>Improve tourist supply | Conservation of a green area and original flora repopulation programme |

| | | | |
|---|---|---|---|
| **L'ESTARTIT (E)** | Creation of the natural protected area of Islas Medas | Public organizations | Reposition on the market<br><br>Diversification of the demand (scuba divers)<br><br>Relaunch of investments<br><br>Seasonal spread out<br><br>Supply of new services for the new visitors | Protection and repopulation of marine fauna<br><br>Availability of new investments for environmental pourpose<br><br>Increase the awareness of local community towards the qualification and preservation of natural resources<br><br>Raise of an environment-oriented attitude |
| | Creation of natural reserve in the Ter Vell lagoon | Public organizations | New opportunities for visiting the area (itineraries)<br><br>Diversification of the demand towards schools a special interest tourists | Protection and qualification of natural space |
| | Environmental education programme for students and alternative tourists | Public organizations | Reinforce the strategy of the resort towards environment qualification | Make tourists an host population more sensitive to environmental issues<br><br>Monitor of the resources |
| | Creation of an information and training centre for marine ecosystem | Public organizations | Reinforce positioning and image of the resort | Diffusion of an environment-conscious itude in the tourists and host populati |

| Location | Project | Operator | Objective | Effects / Notes |
|---|---|---|---|---|
| KNOKKE HEIST (B) | Congress centre | Private operators | Increase off-season tourism / Diversify tourism demand | None / Note: hardly opposed by environmental groups for the localization in a downs area |
| | Tourist harbour +apartments | Private operators | Diversification of the demand (nautical tourism) | Recovery of a deteriorated urban area |
| | Tourist Information Centre | Public-private venture | Improvement of the connection between supply and demand | Make tourists more sensitive towards local resources |
| CORFU' (G) | Creation of a high school for tourism and hotellerie | Private operators | Improvement of the service quality / Elaboration of a relaunch strategy based on a scientific approach | Favourite the integration between tourism culture and local culture |
| | Tourist harbour | Public-private venture | Improvement of the turist supply / Development of new demand segment (nautical tourism) | None |
| | Renewal of historical buildings for cultural/meeting purposes | Public organizations | Requalification of the urban environment | Requalification of the urban environment |
| COSTA SMERALDA - GALLURA (I) | Construction of 2 new tourist resorts (residential villages) of huge dimension | Private operators | Increase of accommodation capacity / New opportunities for workers and small entrepreneurs mainly in the building sector | None / Note: hardly opposed by environmental groups (local and national) for the negative effects on natural environment |

# 7. THE TOURISM/ENVIRONMENT RELATIONS SYSTEM

Previous chapters have outlined some of the effects of the tourist system on the environment in the seaside resorts analysed and identified actions and interactions on the part of some agents intervening in this area. This chapter will examine those factors which we believe to be particularly important for tourism development and which take into consideration environmental aspects. These comments will be taken up again in later chapters when the general guidelines to action are indicated.

## 7.1. INTERPRETATIVE MODELS OF THE RELATIONSHIPS BETWEEN TOURISM AND ENVIRONMENT

This research has from the beginning used a life-cycle model for the tourist resorts in order to interpret the system of relations between tourism development and environmental resources in a seaside resort. The interpretative paradigm of the resort cycle is based on Butler (1980) and has become widely used to describe the temporal or spatial evolution of a tourist resort. According to the author, tourist resorts can be divided according to six distinct phases in their growth process: exploration, involvement, development, consolidation, stagnation, decline-revitalisation. Each of these phases should correspond to specific levels of demand, to different levels of service and involvement on the part of local and external agents and thus different impacts on the environment system.

The present research is concentrated in particular on resorts which are at the turning point of the stagnation and the decline-revitalisation phase. Measurement was carried out by referring to total earnings rather than to number of tourists in order to avoid spurious conclusions (for example, decrease in the number of tourists at the same time as an increase in average spending). This meant that all or almost all our cases shared a situation in which the local tourist economy had begun to show signs of weakness, of economic stagnation or loss of competitivity. The areas were thus in a phase in which the resources available for investment (whether in environmental resources or not) and in general the opportunities present in the area were on the decline.

The following chart shows the various phases of the life cycle of a resort and the implications for environmental resources according to the authors.

## STAGES AND INDICATORS OF THE RESORT LIFE CYCLE (BUTLER, 1980)

**Exploration**
- Small numbers of "allocentrics" or "explorers"
- Little or no tourist infrastructure
- Natural or cultural attractions

**Involvement**
- Local investment in tourism
- Pronounced tourist season
- Advertising the destination
- Emerging market area
- Public investment in infrastructure

**Development**
- Rapid growth in visits
- Visitors outnumber residents
- Well-defined market area
- Heavy advertising
- External investment leads to loss of local control
- Man-made attractions emerge to replace
  natural or cultural
- "Mid-centrics" replace explorers and allocentrics

**Consolidation**
- Slowing growth rates
- Extensive advertising to overcome seasonality
  and develop new markets
- "Psychocentrics" attracted
- Residents appreciate the importance of tourism

**Stagnation**
- Peak visitors numbers reached
- Capacity limits reached
- Resort image divorced from the environment
- Area no longer fashionable
- Heavy reliance on repeat trade
- Low occupancy rates
- Frequent ownership changes
- Development peripheral to original developments

**Decline**
- Spatial and numerical decrease in markets
- A move out of tourism; local investment might
  replace abandonment by outsiders
- Tourism infrastructure is run-down and might
  be replaced by other uses

**Revitalisation**
- Completely new attractions replace original lures
  or new natural resources used

As can be noted, there are differences, sometimes relevant, between the various concrete examples which have been analysed and the situation hypothesised by the theoretical model. In some cases (Eastbourne, for example, but also L'Estartit), the fact that the situation was one of maturity did not affect the fact that initiatives were undertaken with the aim of improving the environment system. In others, the early stage of the life cycle of the tourist product was immediately characterised by excessive consumption of environmental resources. The resorts analysed which are in the phase of stagnation or decline have many differences in terms of the initial environment situation, the attention paid towards the problem of the environment and in the resources that are dedicated to safeguarding it. Position on the life-cycle curve thus does not explain adequately the influence of tourism development on environmental resources.

The life-cycle model in itself is simply a hypothetical development path of resorts, a conceptual model and one which cannot be applied mechanically to real resorts (Haywood, 1986). This inadequacy of the life-cycle model in terms of its ability to explain specific situations (an inadequacy that limits its predictive powers - Cooper and Jackson, 1989) is due to the fact that the duration and intensity of the various phases can vary considerably from case to case according to the interaction of the factors and agents involved. In other words, the variables used (intensity and duration) in order to describe the life-cycle stage of a resort are expressed on a relative scale (market size and age of the resort) while the importance of the "environmental question" requires measurement on an absolute scale.

J. Krippendof (1987) considers the relationship between tourism development and environment in terms of relations between external agents (economic agents and tourists) and local resources (local population and natural environment), seeing them as characterised by a potential unequal exchange in favour of the former. Tourism development, in fact, bring benefits (usually observable in the short term) and costs (usually greater than the benefits and visible only in the medium- and long-term) to local resources. It is only by checking and systematically planning the balance between these counterposed interests that the system of tourism-environment relations can be resolved. The resort life cycle paradigm is useful, but only in indicating the moments of disequilibrium. The stagnation-decline phase is one in which the costs for the local environment emerge clearly, often at a moment when there is no longer any chance, either in physical or economic terms, of repairing the damage done in the expansion phase.

In *Maintaining the Balance* (1991), the "Tourism and Environment" Task Force set up the following triangular model with regard to the main relationships between tourism and the environment:

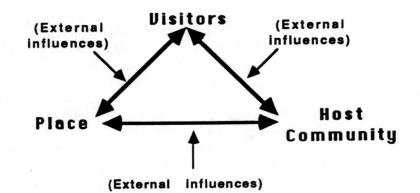

(from Task Force "Tourism and Environment",1991)

This model summarises particularly well the various elements which make up the tourism-environment problem:

- the tourists (which vary in number, demand, behaviour etc.)
- the place (which varies in terms of capacity, presence of natural resources, historical attractions etc.)
- the residents (which vary as regards greater or lesser degrees of openness to tourist development, capacity to benefit from the results of tourist business, etc.)

These three elements are present in all situations and it is the variation of these features from case to case which modifies their interaction. There are also other factors that vary from case to case and which contribute to the modification of the type and intensity of the relations between these basic elements. This model does not take into consideration directly these dynamic aspects.

In the light of these models and of the situations that emerge from our case studies, we will attempt to formulate a more elaborate interpretative framework. It is our view that it is necessary to preserve the dynamic aspect provided by the life-cycle curve, but at the same time to consder other elements such as the characteristics of specific situations, the conditions and the agents on a local level, external forces and the interaction between all these elements which, as we have seen, are discriminating elements in terms of the impact of the environmental resources.

The analysis undertaken in preceding chapters highlighted certain factors which may help in attempting to make some generalisations about the system of tourism-environment relations in the seaside tourist resorts.

It is worth remembering that the research was limited to seaside resorts in phases of maturity or decline. The reason behind this caveat is clear: we are dealing here with large-scale tourism whose development has often taken place at the expense of environmental resources (natural, artificial and cultural). For these resorts, the problem of restoring (or safeguarding) the environment is closely linked to that of revitalising a declining economy. The following considerations are thus valid for these situations alone and cannot necessarily be generalised.

The analysis has identified three groups of agents important for their action on the environmental system of the resorts:

**A) THE MARKET**: this group includes agents on the demand side (tourists) and the intermediary economic agents (tour operators, airline companies), but also those of the supply side (managers of businesses involved in tourism directly as well as those involved indirectly in service industries, as estate agents etc.) The dominance of certain groups and certain agents over others determines the mode of tourism development and the supply model of each resort - more or less capital intensive, more or less "environment consuming".

Four principal types of situations can be identified:

1. NON ORGANIZED DEMAND-LABOUR INTENSIVE SUPPLY
This situation is characterised by small tourist firms with high labour intensity. These account for the classic tourist resorts which grew up in the nineteenth century. Low capital requirements favoured the growth of local family enterprises which even today control the management and sale of the tourist product. These resorts, even with the arrival of mass tourism, have not substantially changed their type of supply or approach to the market. This is probably because of the inadequacy of the existing structures in terms of guaranteeing the necessary profit levels to external agents and because of the high cost of transforming these structures. There is no single holiday type offered, but the individual nature of the demand tends to prioritise the importance of discovery, curiosity, and in general emphasis on non-mass resources.

The capacity of these systems to keep a check on their impact on the environment would seem to be higher due to:
* high competition between private agents, which provides an obstacle to the entry of new agents and the indiscriminate growth of new structures which might provide competition;

* the birth of a systemic vision of the area on the part of the agents involved, which has led to forms of associationism for the sharing of certain costs, the restoration of some parts of the urban fabric, the provision of new services;

- the presence of strong social and familial bonds between the operators and the residents, which tend to prevent the residents' city from being totally subordinated to the tourist city;

- the possibility of manoeuvring management parameters (price, length of the season, demand type, income), making them non-obligatory.

The model is fairly rigid from a structural point of view but can be modified in organisational terms.

## 2. NON ORGANIZED DEMAND-CAPITAL INTENSIVE SUPPLY

This is characterised by residential tourist areas and the spread of holiday homes. This model encourages almost exclusively property companies and commercial businesses, but no real local tourist bourgeoisie emerges. The burden on the area is usually very high, both in terms of the per capita consumption of space typical of this tourism model and the considerable imbalance between the public services necessary to the system and their low level of use. In these cases it is usually major property capital, of external origin, that pressurizes the area to reach the maximum possible level of exploitation. The fact that the direct benefits for the local community (income on property, income from building labour and commerce) are directly proportional to the extension of urban space lead to a situation in which there is no encouragement to the local population to exercise any control over or to put any limit on the use of the resources of the area.

## 3. ORGANIZED DEMAND-CAPITAL INTENSIVE SUPPLY

The dominance of organised demand tends to emphasise the importance of tour operators, of the major tourist flows and thus, on the supply side, an intensive and standardised model: the construction of relatively rigid structures and infrastructures which are able, because of their size and organisation, to guarantee adequate profit levels (at least till the maturity phase). In these cases, the ownership/managment of the tourist and auxiliary structures may be external to the area but also in some cases in the hands of local residents. In both cases, the oligopolistic nature of the demand (and in particular of the channels) exercises strong pressure on the agents directly and indirectly involved in tourism to adapt capacity, prices and service levels to the volume and level of profits foreseen. The kind of holiday that becomes dominant in this case is the classic, highly artificial sun-sand-sea holiday. Motivation to give greater weight to natural and cultural resources are almost entirely lacking. The capacity of the tourist system to limit itself internally is relatively low due to the high degree of dependency on external forces.

## 4. ORGANIZED DEMAND-LABOUR INTENSIVE SUPPLY

This is as yet a model which has been little developed. Only in few places (in particular Rimini) have real situations conforming to this pattern been identified (Unioncamere, 1992). These are small clusters of small tourist businesses under the control of a single firm. This model, which is an organisational evolution of case 1, would seem to permit:

- the achievement of economies of scale usually to be found in larger structures;

- access to organised demand, although this is most likely to be with small, medium-sized or specialised tour operators;
- greater flexibility in terms of the management of the area, modifying objectives and the use of structures to the particular state of demand.

This model would indeed appear to constitute an evolution of the supply system capable of guaranteeing, by means of greater flexibility, less damage on the environment.

Fig. 7.1 presents the four cases described above.

| Supply \ Demand | organised | individual |
|---|---|---|
| **labour intensive/ family enterprise** | *Small accomodation groupings: consortia, clusters*<br><br>Channel: small/specialised Tour Operators | *Diffuse model: small accommodation facilities*<br><br>Old resorts<br><br>Channel: direct, individual or consortium-mediated |
| **capital intensive** | *Intensive model: medium and large accomodation facilities*<br><br>Recent resorts<br><br>Channel: large TO's | *Residential villages Holidays homes*<br><br><br>Channel: real estate agencies |

There is a specific relation between these market types and the environment: the environment constitutes the original resource which gives rise to tourism but tends to be subordinate to the impact of the market, to be used, and thus transformed, according to:

- the prevailing model
- the action of other factors which will be listed later (cfr. 7.3)

For many of the coastal resorts analysed, the environment has been transformed from the sufficient resource to an auxiliary element in relation to tourism due to excessive consumption of environmental resources. For some of these resorts, the degradation of the environment has led to a decrease in competitivity and thus a transformation of the parameters of the market (price, demand segment, profit levels etc.) There is also, then, a feed-back relation between environment and the market in that environmental change (positive or negative) tends to result in modifications to the market, changing demand and supply agents in accordance with the environmental situation of the resort.

The market block also interacts with the resident block.

75

**B) RESIDENTS**: the second block is that of the residents. This relates to the market block in that it is in overall terms a beneficiary of the increase in wealth and services brought by tourism development. Part of the resident population contributes directly (this, then, is the feed-back with the market) to the process of tourist production on several levels varying from:
- mere labour in the construction sector
- employment in the productive processes
- the management of supply structures (regarding tourism and services in general)
- direct control of access channels to demand

The different levels of involvement tend to lead to a polarisation of the resident population into those benefitting from tourism (with part of their overall income deriving from activity involving tourism) and those not benefitting (with income deriving from activities unrelated to tourism).

There are also specific relations between residents and the environment. Indeed, in one sense they are part of the environment, as they are the bearers of the culture, traditions and identity of the area. On the other hand, they should be those responsible for safeguarding the environmental conditions in that they are part of the community permanently exposed to its state and its degradation.

The material that we have collected, however, does not conclusively confirm this relationship. In these kinds of resorts, the benefits brought by tourism create a widespread solidarity with the market block that is vastly greater than any care for the environment. Even those residents not involved in tourism seem to be no more concerned with the negative effects tourism can have on the environment than those directly involved.

The conditions tend to interact in turn with the population (feed-back) in that they determine directly the capacity of the residents to pass on to future generations of the area environmental resources which are at least equal to those they received. There is thus a circularity of interaction between the residents and the environment which highlights potential imbalances (often temporal) between the advantages and disadvantages of tourism development. Those who suffer the damage caused by the degradation of environmental resources provoked by the market, then, are the same people who benefitted from the market in the first place.

## C) THE GOVERNMENT
The government has, institutionally speaking, the task of regulating and improving the various aspects involved in the environment and the reciprocal interaction between:
- the urban system (building projects, traffic, public services)
- the natural system (water, green areas, fauna, flora, etc.)
- the cultural system (schools, museums, traditions, history, etc.)

The impact of the government on the environmental system is thus both direct (when it promotes initiatives aimed at improvement) and indirect (when it fixes limits and regulates the impact of other agents).

As has been pointed out, this regulatory function is often absent or slow. Interventions are made only after long-term damage has put an end to tourism development. The main problem is that as the local government is an expression of the local population (and is, indeed, elected by it), and it thus finds it difficult to renounce the immediate benefits that tourism brings, above all when this appears to be, as often happens, a means of escaping from economic marginality (the case of most of the seaside resorts). In this situation, priority is given to the economic advantages of tourism and no a priori limits are put to its growth, trust being put instead in the self-regulation of the system.

**But neither the market block nor the local population appear to be capable of giving birth to major iniatives aimed at self-regulating environmental resources. This task can and must be carried out by government organisations alone in the first stage and in cooperation with the economic actors at a later stage.**

It is thus necessary that environmental planning (the definition of limits to building programmes, to numbers of tourists, the definition of protected natural areas etc.) should be carried out under the control/supervision of a government organisation (regional, national or of the EEC) less exposed to electoral and economic pressures than local governments.

It is within these limits that the market can find the most profitable and useful economic environment in which to work. Under a clear and well-defined environmental policy umbrella promoted by the (local) government even economic operators can start autonomous processes (functional interventions, re-definition of marketing mix and cooperation between private operators) to make their businesses coherent with the environmental policy of the area.

Fig. 7.2 shows the tourism-environment model as it has been redefined on the basis of this analysis.

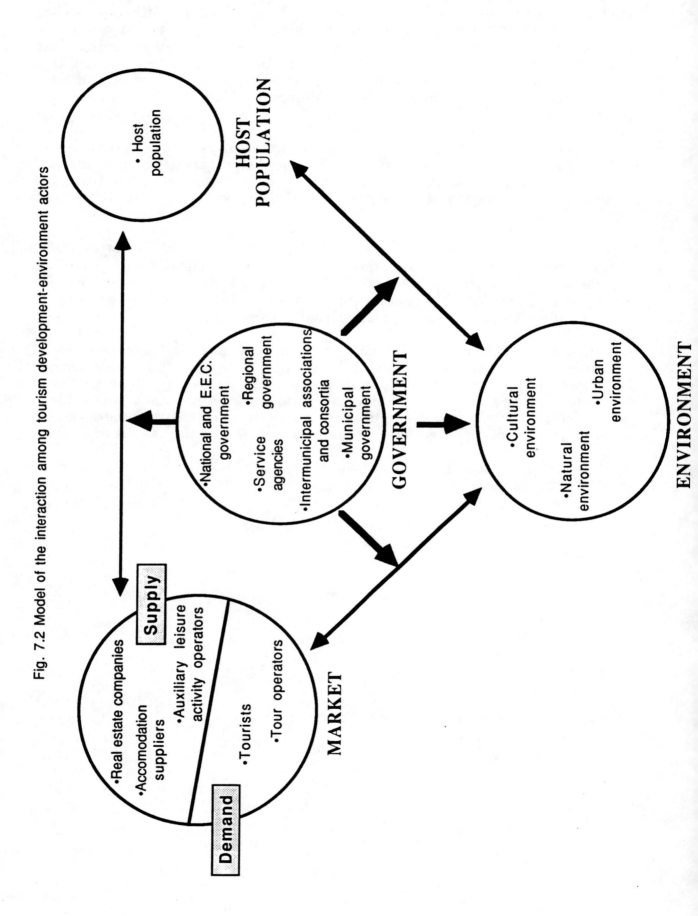

Fig. 7.2 Model of the interaction among tourism development-environment actors

**HOST POPULATION**

• Host population

**GOVERNMENT**

•National and E.E.C. government  •Regional government  •Service agencies  •Intermunicipal associations and consortia  •Municipal government

**ENVIRONMENT**

•Cultural environment  •Natural environment  •Urban environment

**MARKET**

Supply

•Real estate companies  •Accomodation suppliers  •Auxilliary leisure activity operators

Demand

•Tourists  •Tour operators

The interaction model relates to other factors as well, some of which influences the relationships, other which are influenced by them, other still independent of them. These factors are important indicators of the environment wellbeing of a resort.

## 1. The Intensity of Tourism
The resort life-cycle curve indicates growth by focusing on trends in terms of volume of tourists compared to the highest number of tourists found in a resort over a long period of time. The situation of the environment, on the other hand, is of importance almost exclusively only if measured in terms of the absolute burden that a resort is subject to in brief periods (or, at least, in terms of relative burden in comparison to local capacities).

The impact of thousands and thousands of tourists, concentrated, moreover, in a few weeks of the year, inevitably puts environmental resources under stress, even if the resort in which this takes place is structured to cope with even higher numbers of tourists. In resorts accustomed to dealing with large numbers, environmental resources may be greately damaged independently of the phase of the life cycle of the resort, making any sort of improvement very difficult.

On the other hand, the cases in which the numbers of tourists is not high in absolute terms (or compared with the capacity of the resort), the fact that a resort is in the maturity or declining phase does not necessarily indicate a negative environmental situation, in which case a process of renovation may turn out to be less problematic.

Guidelines for action:
• *keep the tourist burden within limits and under control*, under the capacity level of the resort, and facilitate initiatives aimed at making tourist activity <u>less seasonal</u>.

## 2. The "time factor"
The time factor is equally important for environmental resource considerations in tourism development. As we have seen, this variable may have a decisive influence on the evolution of the supply system and may thus affect the tourism - environment system of relations in various ways.

### a) *The assimilation of tourist culture*
Development always involves upsetting economic, social and cultural equilibria. The resolution of a social "crisis" and the reaching of new equilibria require time during which the tourist culture is digested by the pre-existing local culture (usually based on agriculture, fishing and crafts), a class of economic agents tied to tourism arises, and new social alliances take shape. This process, which is essential if tourism is to be accepted and managed successfully, took place in the older resorts over a period of decades, and conflicts were resolved also thanks to the fact that new models were only introduced slowly.

Today, the speed of these processes is incomparably faster. There is no time to incorporate or defend resorts from the impact of this "invasion", or even render the process smoother. In the most recent holiday resorts (Corfù, Cyprus, Turkey) this has given rise to particularly serious imbalances and difficulties in the approach and management of this "new" industry, with important negative repercussions on the natural environment and on the residents themselves.

For the time factor, too, the relative measurement of these phenomena, then, does not lead to a greater understanding of the situation. It is only with respect to absolute time and the length of the various phases that the life-cycle model may lead to a better understanding of the tourism - environment relationship.

Guidelines for action:
• fast growth is one of the requirements for the external agents (tour operators, hotel chains, airline companies, financing groups), responding to pressing short-term profit demands, but not for the local community which has to move in a long-term perspective, undertaking local initiatives that tend to slow down growth rates with the aim of assimilating new models.

b. *Rigidity with regard to change in the supply system*
The dominant model of tourist demand in the time (absolute time again) when the seaside resorts develop seem to "imprint" the features of the supply structure which is virtually unchanging even in the near future.

In cases in which the resort has begun to develop on the basis of an individual tourist demand (Eastbourne, Knokke Heist and Rimini, for example) a family-type entrepreneurship has arisen, giving rise to a prevalently labour-intensive supply characterised by medium or low capital requirements. Although the characteristics of the tourist market have changed over time (both in demand and in supply and distribution), these resorts have not changed substantially but, at the most, have elaborated strategies based on the modernising of the original supply model. The reasons for this are:

-   the inadequate nature of the structures and infrastructures for the new productivity parameters
-   the high cost of adaptation
-   the deep-rooted nature of the system of relations between the agents involved

In the case of Rimini, for example, the coming of the era of the big international tour operators has given rise neither to the entry of external investors nor to a radical shift towards organised tourism (as happened, for example, in Cyprus - Ioannides, 1992). Instead, there has been a growth of forms of cooperation between tourism facilities and auxiliary services, hotel groupings, service sharing and other innovations which allow a critical mass to be reached with respect to production costs and marketing while maintaining high flexibility. These initiatives have helped maintain the competitivity of the resort, threatened by the entry of new supply models on the market, at an acceptable level (in terms of price, quality and services).

The dominant tourist supply and demand models in the last few decades in seaside resorts prioritise the achievement of economies of scale by means of the construction of large structures, themselves excessively rigid with respect to a possible re-use in the future. The rigidity of the system with regard to change, together with the functional rigidity of the structure leads to strict limits to any possible requalification of the environment or the tourism of a resort.

Guidelines for action:
• the imposition of *flexibility criteria* on the planning of tourist structures and infrastructure within urban planning as a whole. The ability of future generations to reconvert these structures and infrastructures according to the various requirements of the demand is vital to the legitimacy of tourism development.

### 3. Autonomy of the residents in the process of production/sales
An important factor that determines the state of relations between tourism and environment is the level of control over the production of  tourist services exercised by the local residents.

The extent of involvement of the local community may vary:
- from the simple provision of labour for building
- to employment in the productive process
- to the management of supply structures
- to direct control of access channels to demand (or at any rate to independence from the large oligopolistic companies).

Each of these levels entails a different degree of autonomy as regards the management of the area, and particularly in terms of a capacity to control development endogenously (it is clear that in general the logic of the external agent subordinates the interests of the local community to profit motivations).

The results of this research in this area are clear. Regulation of growth processes, in various forms, exists only in cases in which residents have a degree of autonomy in the management of the supply structures (*how to manage*) and contemporaneously in those of selling (*how to sell*).

Where the local population participates in tourism development almost exclusively by providing labour for building (this is the case of the Costa Esmeralda in Sardinia), there are no limits to the growth of structures or infrastructures because these would lead the source of income and wealth to dry up. The same is true when  para-tourist models dominate (second homes). Here, indeed, the interest of the local population is to continue expansion.

Even in those cases in which the local community manages tourist activity but depends almost entirely on the major international tour operators for the access to demand (this is the case of Lloret de Mar and Corfù), development takes place without any control. The pressure brought to bear by the external agents (tour operators and airline companies) is very heavy and pushes towards the intensive exploitation of the greatest possible area available. Unlike the previous case, however, there is a greater distribution of wealth amongst the local community.

Only in cases in which the local community participates in the whole  tourist process (production and sales) do limits to uncontrolled growth begin to appear.  This does not mean necessarily that in these cases there is a higher sense of environmental issues. There is rather a defence of income and of corporate interests, so that any change to the status quo is seen as a potential danger, any expansion of supply is seen as an increase in competition which must be blocked. This same situation can give rise on the other hand to processes of product diversification and innovation that do not usually occur when the major external agents control important parts of the tourist trade (see also Debbage, 1990).

In cases in which there is high autonomy on the part of residents, there is usually also a high respect for the appearance of the environment and the city. These resorts were often the first to undertake investments in the purification of reflux water and in the collection and processing of rubbish.

Guidelines for action:
• encourage the control of the local community over the management of tourism resources


## 4) Social and economic conditions

Another very important macro-variable in determining the relations between tourism development and the environment is the social and economic conditions on which tourism development is based. Advanced economic and social conditions (in terms of income, economic structure, administrative efficiency or simply the existence of a strong cultural identity) give the resident community (and its adminsistrators) greater negotiating power vs. the agents of tourism development, compared to underdeveloped areas. They are also less subordinated to the logic of the promoters of tourism development. This is true both for the take-off phase (which takes place, however, always in subordinate economic areas) and phases of rejuvenation.

Another factor which helps to avoid dependence on the often severe logic of indiscriminate tourism development is the diversification of the local economy, the strengthening of the presence of sectors which are independent of the tourism cycle. Diversification, if present in the socio-economic system of the area, can affect the mode of tourism development. It can give resorts not only the option of whether or not to accept the opportunities offered by the tourist industry but above all the chance to influence its forms and objectives, of controlling, that is, its impact on the environment system.

Guidelines for action:
• avoiding the transformation of tourism development into the activity which dominates the economic base of the area
• maintaining pre-existing business activity and encouraging the siting of businesses which are compatible with but independent of tourism and which can act as alternatives.


## 5) The environment as a factor of attraction

A final factor which emerges from our research as crucial to the relationship between tourism and the environment is the importance of environmental features in the tourist image of the resort. The more the environment (in the form of nature parks, centres of historical and cultural interest etc.) is used as an important qualifiying factor in terms of services and auxiliary activities, the more it becomes an economic factor *per se* and is thus perceived as necessary to the reproduction of the system. This process, however, clearly needs limits and a conscious planning and control on the part of public authorities in order to avoid difficulties arising in terms of the maintenance of an equilibrium between economic interests and those of safeguarding the environment.

An interesting case in this respect is that of L'Estartit, where several islands near the resort have made themselves into a nature park. In this case, the publicising of the high environmental-ecological importance of the area modified tourist demand but also changed the perception of the residents and local agents of the environment, although this took place over a longer period of time, time that is necessary for the verification of the economic attractiveness of this new situation. The environment became the principal tourist resource, as it had been in the original phase of its life cycle, a sufficient factor of attraction. The difference, in this case, is that the awareness of the need to safeguard this resource spread to the local government, the resident population and even to those directly involved in tourism. This gave rise to regulation, previously absent, and the fixing of clear limits to growth, with the aim of giving greater value to the natural environment and at the same time to its exploitation for tourist aims.

## 6) The resort life cycle

The life-cycle curve also plays an important part in the model, but a *sui generis* role compared to the others. The position of a resort on the life-cycle curve is not particularly useful in terms of describing the environmental situation. This, we believe, depends substantially on the five factors mentioned above. It does, however, indicate the availability of private capital for interventions in resorts (whether these regard the environment or not). In the maturity phase of the life cycle, in fact, returns on investment become smaller and capital begins to shift towards more profitable investments. The decline phase is thus characterised by difficulties in terms of access to new financial resources due to the insufficiency of local financial resources and the unattractiveness of the resort for external investors due to the low return on investment. It is thus in the introduction and development phases that the profit levels are high and that financial resources are available for interventions which can also be, we believe, directed at the environment. In the situation of maturity and decline, then, we are faced with the whole problem of how and where to find the capital resources necessary to revitalise the resort and to make it sufficiently attractive to investors to begin (or continue) the process of improving the environment.

The factors listed here are, in the light of our research, those which have the greatest influence on the state of environmental resources and are thus those which determine the probability of success of attempts to improve the environment system or to avoid its further impoverishment.

# 8. RECOMMENDATIONS FOR THE ACTION

Following the research carried out, certain operative guidelines have emerged which we retain of primary importance and should be taken into consideration in any attempt to improve the condition of the environment in the course of tourism development.

The guidelines proposed do not make specific mention of all the innumerable protective and recuperative environmental measures which could be taken: these are so numerous that it would be useless to reiterate them and, moreover, their effects are so general that they cannot be limited to the area of tourism (for example, limiting traffic or saving energy). Excellent check-lists already exist which identify the most appropriate measures for tourism development compatible with the environment (Studienkreis fur Tourismus, 1991).

On the contrary, these are operative objectives to be taken into account in the management of tourism development.

For each objective the following are given:
- a brief description
- the motivation of the action (WHY)
- some measures which can be applied in order to achieve it (HOW)
- the actors responsible for the action (promotors and executors) (WHO)
- the subjects to whom the action is addressed (TO WHOM)
- a subjective evaluation of the effectiveness (i.e. in improving the situation)
- a subjective evaluation of the efficiency (i.e. the likelihood of achieving the objective given the resources)
- an estimate of the time scale necessary for its application (short vs. long term)

| Objective 1.  *The area as system* |

Coordinate services and economically productive processes in order to arrive at a systemic supply.  Define development strategies which take into account the territorial and functional coordination of resources.  Ascertain in advance the advantages offered by the interventions and to examine the results achieved during the course of the interventions: a strategic approach allows the flexibility to adapt to a changing context.

| Why |

The quality of the environment as perceived by tourists and residents may not be defined in isolation but is connected with numerous other factors:  natural resources, but also socio-cultural, urban, artistic and historical ones, etc.  The quality of the environment depends simultaneously and interdependently on all of these.

The development policies of government and planning bodies do not follow an integrated approach.  A policy geared to the environment, on the other hand, involves the understanding and consideration of all the factors involved in development, of their interrelation and different rates of evolution and of their varying impact on the environment.

| How |

- setting up information and productive networks to make the bodies involved more aware of the resources and reciprocally integrated

- analysis of costs and benefits and environmental audits; compulsory consideration of the environmental impact for tourism projects

- analysis of the macro-economic scenario to take into account direct and indirect effects, in the short and especially the long term

- procedures for coordination between various departments (economic development, the environment, tourism, town planning, culture) of local and regional government

- encouraging coordination between economic operators

- medium-term planning for growth and development at area-system level

| Who |

Local governments (regional, town councils) tourist boards, service agencies

Primarily public bodies but also private economic operators.

Effectiveness: high     Efficiency: low     Time scale: long

| Objective 2a | *Strengthen control at supra-local level* |
|---|---|

Prevent decisions on regulation and planning being taken at a purely local level. Make environmental protection policies dependent on non-local strategies and equilibria (at least at regional level).

## Why

Local governments may not be the most diligent in avoiding excessive land use and pursuing a policy of environmental protection: the local population, who are the first to benefit economically from tourism development, may exert great pressure (political and electoral) on the local government.

It is therefore vital that development limits are set by a level of government which is not so vulnerable to immediate local interests.

## How

- regional level planning for the protection of the environment

## Who

National and Regional governments

## To whom

Town councils

## Evaluation

Effectiveness:medium    Efficiency: high    Time scale: short

NB   Effectiveness is greatest when combined with Objective 2b.

| Objective 2b | *Limit accommodation capacity* |
| --- | --- |

To establish limits to the growth of accommodation capacity, if possible at an intermediate stage in the resort life cycle. This objective can be achieved particularly in the context of planning measures at regional level (Objective 2a).

## Why

It is the supply which must establish desirable limits compatible with development. Limits on development should preferably be imposed by a level of government which is not subject to local interests.

## How

- establishing acceptable and compatible development objectives
- agreeing limits on development (usually in terms of number of beds and building permission)

## Who

Local governments (regional, town councils).

## To whom

Private economic operators

## Evaluation

Effectiveness: high     Efficiency:high          Time scale: short

| Objective 3 | *Coordination between entities influencing environment resources* |

Combine public and private strategies and interventions in order to protect and improve recognisable homogeneous parts of the environmental system.

## Why

The heterogeneous nature of environmental resources means that their protection and improvement is sometimes the responsibility of both public and private bodies. Even when the resource comes under the control of public bodies (the sea, natural parks, public urban areas, etc), there are usually private operators working in the area in an economic capacity. There is frequently a difference of interests: on the one hand, gaining the maximum profit from tourism; on the other, avoiding environmental destruction.

## How

- by creating partnerships or public-private bodies (associations or committees) to establish regulations for the use, capacity and consumption of homogeneous environmental areas (the beach, the sea, urban areas, museums, etc), which we shall call <u>environmental clusters.</u>

Private individuals operating within these clusters would participate in these bodies (fishermen for the sea, bathing establishment operators for the beach) as well as representatives from environmental groups.

The aims of these bodies would be:

- to agree on general guidelines and measures for balanced development and utilisation of the environmental cluster;

- to establish rules and regulations for tourist use, accommodation and behaviour in the cluster;

- to assess and propose modifications to the local governments's planning and development projects insofar as these affect that environmental cluster.

## Who

Local governments (regional, town councils)

## To whom

Private economic operators, Environmental groups, Local groups and committees

## Evaluation

Effectiveness: medium    Efficiency: medium    Time scale: long

## Objective 4  *Limitation of peaks and seasonal spreading*

Avoid excessive crowding in high season -- and during the weekend -- and redistribute the tourist flow throughout the year (high/low season trade-off). The achievement of a trade-off is essential and involves not only increasing off-season activity but also reducing peak period use.

## Why

Tourist demand based on high seasonal concentration (high peaks in the summer and sporadic demand during the rest of the year) tends to be environment-consuming.

A high seasonal peak produces various negative effects:

1   the environment is subject to intense stress and over-use.  This situation is more difficult to control than a constantly high use.

2   there is a high risk of outbursts of saturation and intolerance unforseeable by tourists or residents

3   urban and specifically tourist structures and infrastructures may follow different use patterns:
    a)  beyond saturation point in peak periods but also high  in other periods (taken on an annual average)
    b)  decidedly low (based on a seasonal high)

    The situation described in (b) is far more widespread and implies:

    - cost to the community of administration and maintenance of services and infrastructures which remain unused for the greater part of the year

    - low return on investment

4   quality of service drops in the face of excessive demand.  In fact, less qualified seasonal workers are employed to cope with peak demand.

## How

Tourist Management measures may help to control and limit tourist numbers in high season (see also Tourism and the Environment Task Force, 1991 and ETB 1992).

The following in particular may be potentially most effective for the resorts under consideration:

- increasing prices for accommodation and ancilliary services
- increasing airport taxes
- limiting private traffic
- limiting the size of car parks

These measures tend to discourage the resident tourist using the aforementioned accommodation but have little effect on daily visitors, who often represent a greater problem.

As far as extending the season is concerned, this is a question which all tourist resorts have started to address, though sometimes only in its most conservative form, i.e. "purely additional demand".

Measures which may assist seasonal redistribution have been identified in relation to the following areas:

Business tourism (during the week)
- creating a conference centre
- creating a trade fair area
- diversifying the economic structure of the area

Special interest tourism (weekends)
making the most of the area for the following:
- culture (art exhibitions, historical buildings and remains, museums, etc)
- nature (inland areas, rural tourism, green areas)
- food and wine
- sporting and other events

Obviously, the feasibility of each of these options will vary according to local conditions and resources.

| Who |
| --- |

Local governments (regional, municipal) and private economic operators

| To whom |
| --- |

Private economic operators and tourists.

| Evaluation |
| --- |

Effectiveness:high    Efficiency:low    Time scale: long

Make residents perceived environmental quality as an economic opportunity. Use the concept of environmental quality in communication and promotion initiatives.

## Why

In localities where it is environmental factors - natural, historical, cultural - which are the main factors emphasised in marketing the area and therefore the main source of business (natural parks, areas of great historical or traditional value), the need to operate in an environmentally friendly way is largely accepted by businesses and residents. In such cases, the preservation of the environment becomes the guarantee of future business.

Obviously, not all tourist destinations can base their future marketing on valuable environmental attractions but it is possible to achieve a certain harmony and freedom from overcrowding even in an artificial context and to re-position it on the market from this viewpoint.

## How

Product improvement:
- improvement programmes for urban and natural areas
- use of building materials and technology in keeping with th environment
- visitor management (limiting road traffic, parking, noise, etc)
- re-cycling, re-using  programmes
- controlling and limiting the discharge of pollutant waste in air and water
- creating networks for the coordination of resources

Marketing:
- definition of an environment-saving strategy
- use of the concept of environmental quality in promotional initiatives
- publicising measures carried out

## Who

Local governments (regional, municipal), private economic operators, tourist boards

## To whom

Private economic operators, tourists, host population.

## Evaluation

Effectiveness:high     Efficiency:high    Time scale:long

## Objective 6  *Emphasize local identity*

Preserve and make the most of local traditions and culture. Emphasize local identity and avoid standardisation.

### Why

Especially in small communities, the development of tourism frequently suppresses or pushes aside the local culture and imposes outside building styles and patterns of behaviour which are totally alien to the local character. Excessive standardisation by large business organisations tends to create a "could be anywhere" resort.

### How

- making it compulsory to use local styles of building in new construction. Refurbishing existing buildings in the urban fabric

- making the most of and publicising local traditions (culture, cuisine, language) through events advertised to tourists

### Who

Local governments (regional, town councils), Local cultural associations, Tourist boards

### To whom

Host population and tourists.

### Evaluation

Effectiveness:medium    Efficiency:medium    Time scale: short

93

## Objective. 7 *Flexible planning*

Impose design and building criteria which lend themselves to flexibility and future re-conversion.

### Why

Rigid planning concerning structures and infrastructures imposes heavy constraints on any future re-evaluation of tourism and the environment because of the various demands on the hardware and software involved.

### How

- Giving priority to the refurbishment of existing buildings (children's seaside "camps", hotels, etc)
- Avoiding "closed" planning solutions and favouring modular ones which allow for possible future modifications
- Developing networks aimed at different purposes: productive, operative and informative

### Who

Local administration  (regional, town councils).

### To whom

Public bodies and private economic operators.

### Evaluation

Effectiveness: high     Efficiency: low     Time scale: long

NB   Difficult to put into practice.

## Objective 8 *Selection of demand*

Diversify the market niches of tourist demand and move progressively towards those more compatible with local development and resources. Concentrate on those which support environmental improvement.

### Why

A typical "market driven" approach, based on meeting the requirements of the demand and on maximizing consumer satisfaction, leads not to compatible tourism development but merely to quantitative growth.

Tourist demand dominated by a search for the lowest price is not conducive to a supply concentrating on environmental improvement as the environment is a quality product which must be paid for.

Dealing with tourism and the environment, we feel that by waiting for a display of environmental concern on the part of a considerable proportion of consumers, one runs the risk of postponing any action for too long. The demand-dominium paradigm must be reversed or at least mixed: the supply (specifically the bodies managing the territorial resources) must define its objectives in advance, based on a balanced use of resources and therefore addressing itself to the market segments most in line with these objectives (and with the product). It is also possible to "create" discerning consumers in this way, by enabling them to perceive and appreciate the difference.

### How

* Establishing and implementing strategic marketing plans (at resort and micro-structure level), and operative marketing actions selecting and focussing on targets in line with compatible development.

### Who

Local government, Tourist boards.

### To whom

Private economic operators and tourists.

### Evaluation

Effectiveness: high    Efficiency: low    Time scale: long

| Objective 9 | *Encorage autonomy in the production/sale of the tourism product* |

Facilitate the host population's participation in running and advertising the tourist attractions and facilities. Internalise tourism management. Pursue a self-managed development of tourism or a balanced exchanged with outside forces.

### Why

Decision-making coming from outside the area concerning the ownership/management of tourist structures and ways of meeting tourism's demands does not safeguard the environment. On the contrary, it puts pressure on the local environment because such operators tend to force the rate and type of development for speculative reasons. On the other hand, giving the resident population the opportunity of participating in tourism management and publicity would seem to ensure a greater guarantee of compatibility in the development process.

### How

- identifying different market niches and diversifying channels in order to avoid a demand oligopoly
- tourism management training and job creation schemes
- offering financial incentives for the purchase of tourist structures with or without external operators
- the creation of agencies/cooperatives for:
  - access to public funding
  - promotion and publicity for the tourism product
  - access for small businesses to the international market through committees
  - diffusion of know-how
  - refresher courses in technology and the organisation and marketing management

### Who

EEC, Local and national governments, Trade associations and federations, Tourism training colleges and schools

### To whom

Private entrepreneurs.

### Evaluation

Effectiveness: high     Efficiency:medium     Time scale: long

96

Encourage individual operators or groups of operators to adopt environmental measures. as far as their immediate territory is concerned - i.e. their micro-environment (e.g. for a hotelier: the hotel interior, the surrounding urban area, the hotel beach, etc).

## Why

Private operators and the resident population do not generally have a global perception of the environment but only of those parts in which they are directly involved (because they live or work there). A contribution to tourism development which is compatible with the environment must begin with a series of individual actions (a bottom-up process).

It must be clearly perceived by all operators involved that the concept of safeguarding the environment is no longer a moral obligation for future compatible development but is a very real factor affecting the present quality of the tourism product.

## How

- Press/TV/direct mail campaigns on "Why/How to be environmentally friendly ..." aimed at the resident population and the economic operators in the field of tourism: hoteliers, restauranteurs and all the other categories involved
- specific training for operators on:
- why one should adopt environmentally friendly measures in hotels, restaurants and ancilliary structures (because it is economically advantageous as well as morally right)
- how to do this
- how to communicate this and benefit from it
- tax benefits for operators who adopt specific consumption-saving practices
- awards and publicity for those who adopt the most effective measures

## Who

Local governments, Trade associations

## To whom

Private economic operators.

## Evaluation

Effectiveness:medium    Efficiency:medium    Time scale: short

## Objective 11 *Involving the tourists*

Assist the tourist in using and respecting the local resources. Publicise projects undertaken, especially those concerning the environment.

### Why

Tourists usually have minimal involvement in the locality where they spend at most a few weeks in a year. They choose the locality on the basis of their requirements and when a locality no longer satisfies them, they choose another.

They use the land in an intensive rather than extensive manner. Greater understanding of the locality in which they are staying, the projects undertaken by the community and of the regulations in force may lend to greater involvement and greater pleasure.

### How

- information on the reality of the local situation
- advice on how to benefit from the resources available
- directories of projects in general and of environmentally friendly ones in particular
- visitor management program

### Who

Tourist boards, Private economic operators

### To whom

Tourists.

### Evaluation

Effectiveness: medium    Efficiency:medium    Time scale: short

## Objective 12 *Priority for resorts in decline*

Give priority to the recovery of resorts in decline.

### Why

Resorts in the phases of maturity/decline are in situations where the human and capital resources are already high. It is important to give priority to these situations especially with a view to the future in order to avoid losing a valuable collection of resources and to put the local communities involved back into perspective. Successful intervention in these areas could also reduce pressure on areas still to be developed or those unsuitable for tourism development.

The main problem regarding these areas is the lack of access to new sources of funding: insufficient local financial resources combined with limited attraction for outside investors. Financial incentives for interventions in this type of areas can play an important role in the recovery process.

### How

- Financial incentive, particularly for the improvement or upgrading of resorts in the decline phase and for the re-use of obsolete structures.
- Creation of local centres (task forces) combining information/ training/ consultancy to promote increased competitiveness necessary for the improvement of the environment. These centres should:

1) identify, test and promote environment-improving interventions, visitor management, energy saving, recycling, refurbishment of existing buildings, the use of materials and technologies of low environmental impact.

2) develop projects (hardware and software) on environmental issues, designed to create new economic opportunities particularly by means of partnerships with tour operators and outside investors.

3) assist local governments and businesses in strategic planning and improvement.

### Who

EEC, National governments, Service agencies

### To whom

Local governments, Private economic operators, Trade associations and federations, Tourist Boards

### Evaluation

Effectiveness: high   Efficiency: medium   Time scale: long

## Objective 13 *Diffusion of tourism-environment know-how*

Coordinate and promote environmental improvement projects concerned with tourism resources, visitor management, energy saving, recycling, re-use of existing structures, use of materials and technologies of low environment impact.

### Why

Accurate information about regulations, technology available, results of interventions carried out is vital for effective action.

### How

- creating a centralised data-base to publicise the positive and negative results of interventions regarding tourism and the environment
- links with local task forces

### Who

EEC, National tourist boards

### To whom

Local governments, Trade associations and federations, Private economic operators, Service agencies

### Evaluation

Effectiveness:medium    Efficiency:high    Time scale: short

Stimulate environmental improvement projects from the outside by creating competition amongst resorts to produce the best projects and publicising the outcome.

## Why

The resorts concerned can strengthen communication and awareness amongst the public about the environment improvement projects which have been undertaken. The effects of these projects is increased and there is a greater incentive to continue.

## How

- creating periodic merit awards for resorts achieving the best environment improvement results in each tourist product category

- publicising the results

## Who

EEC, National and local tourist boards

## To whom

Local tourism boards, Private economic operators, Trade associations and federations

## Evaluation

Effectiveness:low    Efficiency:medium    Time scale:short

NB   It's difficult to establish objective parameters for such an evaluation system.

# Effectiveness-efficiency matrix for intervention proposals: time scale

Legend: ○ Short term  ● Long term

|  | EFFICIENCY | | |
|---|---|---|---|
| **EFFECTIVENESS** | **low** | **medium** | **high** |
| **high** | ● 1. The area as system<br>● 4. Limitation of peaks and seasonal spreading<br>● 7. Flexible planning<br>● 8. Selection of demand | ● 9. Encourage autonomy in the production/ sale of the tourism product<br>○ 2a. Strengthen government control at supra-local level<br>● 12. Priority for resorts in decline | ○ 2b. Limits to the accommodation capacity<br>● 5. Market the environment |
| **medium** | | ● 3. Coordination between entities influencing environment resources<br>○ 6. Emphasize local identity<br>○ 10. Work at the microscale<br>○ 11. Involving the tourists<br>○ 14. Stimulating environmental competition | ○ 13. Diffusion of tourism-environment know-how |
| **low** | | | |

# Effectiveness-efficiency matrix for intervention proposals: promoting agents

Legend: ● Local/regional government  ◉ National/EEC Government  ○ Private Operators

|  | **EFFICIENCY** | | |
|---|---|---|---|
| **EFFECTIVENESS** | **low** | **medium** | **high** |
| **high** | ●○ 9. Encourage autonomy in the production/sale of the tourism product<br>◉● 2a. Strengthen government control at supra-local level<br>◉ 12. Priority for resorts in decline<br><br>● 1. The area as system<br>●○ 4. Limitation of peaks and seasonal spreading<br>● 7. Flexible planning<br>● 8. Selection of demand | ● 2b. Limits to the accommodation capacity<br>●○ 5. Market the environment | |
| **medium** | ● 3. Coordination between entities influencing environment resources<br>● 6. Emphasize local identity<br>●○ 10. Work at the microscale<br>●○ 11. Involving the tourists<br>◉ 14. Stimulating environmental competition | ◉ 13. Diffusion of tourism-environment know-how | |
| **low** | | | |

The preceding tables summarise the general framework of the interventions proposed in terms of efficiency, efficacy, time-span and agents.

EFFICIENCY/EFFICACY AND REALISATION TIME

Comments

1. Almost all interventions with high degrees of efficacy require long realisation times (objective 2b is an exception here).

2. Very few interventions with low realisation times are efficient.

3. High degrees of efficacy are, usually, low to medium on a scale of efficiency.

Objective 2b (fixing limits to tourist capacity) merits particular attention in that it would seem to be the only one capable of providing solutions in the short term. If this objective is interpreted in the strict sense (for example, laying down rigid parameters regarding the number of beds by means of local legislation), it will be fairly high in terms of efficiency as it will require only a formal decision on the part of the local authority.

However, in general, fixing limits to development requires more than a simple decision regarding building programmes. In fact, in situations where decisions of this nature have been taken, the nature of the relationship (consensus or disagreement) between the body responsible for the decision and the economic agents, and the objectives of the various parties involved concerning development take on particular importance.

EFFICIENCY/EFFICACY AND AGENTS RESPONSIBLE FOR THE REALISATION OF THE INITIATIVES

Comments

The role of the local or regional government in the interventions proposed is crucial, particularly in the more difficult interventions, those in which, in other words, there is high efficacy combined with low efficiency. The cross-analsys of (promoters - clients) of the proposals formulated shows the relations between local governments and private business to the the crucial articulation of the system, and as such has vital consequences on the tourism-environment relationship.

A series of important relationships emerge, amongst which:

  * local government + site operators and tourists

* local government and residents

* local government and higher institutional levels

The EEC plays an important role in the identification of general strategies for compatible development and the diffusion of environmental awareness and innovations in the field.

We have limited the interventions identified to those regarding agents operating in the area itself (site operators), leaving aside those involving other agents also of major importance in determining the nature of tourism development such as tour operators and airline companies.

This has been done deliberately. The latter do not act on an area basis, and as such are not directly subject to measures aimed at regulating activity in line with the environment but rather are affected indirectly by actions undertaken by site operators. For these agents, the adoption of criteria which take into account the environment is an arbitrary action undertaken on the basis of individual marketing strategy. Some of the major tour operators have recently become involved to the matter demonstrating how they can play an important role in the education of the tourist (H. Muller, 1992).

## BASIC BIBLIOGRAPHY

Butler,R.W., *The Concept of a Tourist Area Cycle of Evolution: Implication for anagement of Resources*, Canadian Geographer, 1980

Debbage K, *Oligopoly and the Resort Cycle in the Bahamas*, Annals of Tourism Research, n.4,1990

Econstat. *Tourism and Environmental Crises: the Impact of Algae on Summer Holidays along the Adriatic Riviera in 1989*, Esomar, 1991

English Tourism Board, *The Green Light. A Guide to Sustainable Tourism*, 1992

Globe 90, *An Action Strategy for Sustainable Tourism Development, Vancouver*, 1990

Hamele H., Mantzell M., *More Know-How. More Action. Bricks on an ecologically beneficial tourism development*, Studienkreis fur Tourismus, 1991

Krippendof J., *La-Haut sur la montagne..., Pour un développement du tourisme en harmonie avec l'homme et la nature*, MaB Programme, Berne, 1987

Ioannides D., *Tourism Development Agents. The Cypriot Resort Cycle*, Annals of Tourism Research, n.4,1992

Muller H., *Ecology Management in Tourism: Time is of the Essence*, FIF Berne, 1992

Muller H., *Ecological Product Declaration rather than "green" symbol schemes,*, FIF Berne, 1992

OECD,*L'impact du Tourisme sur l'Environment*, 1980

Rochslitz K.H., *Naturnaher Tourismus - Moglichkeiten und Grenzen*, 1986

Task Force Tourism and the Environment, *Maintaining the Balance* , 1991

UNEP, *Workshop on Environmental Aspects of Tourism*, 1983

WTO, *Consideration of a basic dicument on Tourism and Environment, Amsterdam*, 1990